The Up Side of Being Down

Healing the *Dis-Ease* of Negativity with Mind Fitness

Joy L. Watson

ISBN Paperback: # 979-8-9889746-3-5
ISBN Electronic: # 979-8-9889746-2-8
Library of Congress Control Number: #2024902413

Portions of this book are works of nonfiction. Certain names and identifying characteristics have been changed.

Printed in the United States of America.

Joy L. Watson
www.mindfitnessbooks.com

The author's intent is to offer information of a general nature to help you on your quest for emotional, physical, and psychological well-being. In the event you use any of the information in this book for yourself, the author and the publisher assume no responsibility for your actions. This publication is not intended as a substitute for the advice of a healthcare professional.

For All Who Challenge Their Down Side.

Contents

Author's Note vii

Introduction..ix

Part 1: Who, Me? 1

Chapter 1: Here We Go…..3

Chapter 2: What to Do? Mind Fitness 9

Chapter 3: Every Day? Regular Mental Quiet.............................15

Chapter 4: Benefits? Generosity of Spirit… 21

Chapter 5: Picture This! We Become What We Image 25

Chapter 6: How About a Map? Coping to Creating.....................29

Chapter 7: Want to Try Love? Optimal Living 35

Chapter 8: How Did It Start? The Beginnings…Maybe................39

Chapter 9: Are You Unique? Yep, Custom-Made 45

Chapter 10: Springboard? Down to Up 51

Chapter 11: Where Are You? Symptoms of Dis-Ease..................55

Chapter 12: The Payoffs 73

Chapter 13: Are You Ready? The Three Stages of Healing 77

Chapter 14: Scared? The Moment of Decision..........................83

Part 2: Let's Go! Mind Fitness for Healing 87

Chapter 15: A Quiet Place..89

Chapter 16: Why Relax?..93

Chapter 17: A Relaxation Story 97

Chapter 18: In Your Mind's Eye Visualize 101

Chapter 19: It's All Yours! 107

Chapter 20: Why Affirm? 115

Chapter 21: It's for You! Make the Words Your Own......................... 119

Chapter 22: What's the Timing? Rhythm and Style 125

Chapter 23: Prepping for Your "No Sweat" Workout........................ 129

Chapter 24: Seven Easy Parts 133

Chapter 25: Two Stories: Joan and Ben 143

Part 3: Building Steady Attitudes...147

Chapter 26: Positive Momentum Images and Techniques................. 149

Chapter 27: You Are in Charge! Techniques That Work.................... 155

Chapter 28: More Techniques That Work: Negativity Breakers......... 163

Chapter 29: How Are You Treating You? Kindness to Ourselves 169

Chapter 30: "You're So Fine!" Self-Acknowledgment 175

Recommended Books...181

Discussion Questions..183

About The Author 185

Author's Note

THIS IS A new edition of the original book, *The Up Side of Being Down: It's About Your Attitude.* I have given this new edition the subtitle *Healing the Dis-Ease of Negativity,* the title under which I originally wrote the book. Dis-Ease, with the emphasis on the word "ease," refers not to an illness per se but describes the discomfort and uneasiness we experience when consumed by a downward attitude and thinking pattern.

Twenty years ago, I thought it was too pointed to put the word negativity on the cover, so I softened the subtitle to *It's About Your Attitude.* Times have changed, and we are more openly discussing negative attitudes in our society. Thus, *Healing the Dis-Ease of Negativity* more accurately reflects this book's content.

The Up Side is that we can change this negative downward way of viewing life. We can change being on the Down Side of life. Healing our personal negativity with Mind Fitness guides us to recognize and accept our individual forms of negative thinking as the beginning step to healing that unwanted downward, on-the-edge feeling.

This guide was the first in what has grown to be the Mind Fitness Series. This initial book deals with the below-the-line negativity in our lives.

The second book, *From Stress to Sanity: It's About the Way You Think,* deals with our life stresses. It is above-the-line thinking that encourages us to reach our full potential.

The third and newest book, *Mind Fitness: A Guide to Elevating Mental Health,* addresses our recent mental health crisis. It offers a way of viewing our mental fitness and leads readers in self-inquiry exercises to thrive in their well-being.

All three advocate putting mental fitness on the same footing as physical fitness and suggest learning exercises to guide you. They offer valuable roadmaps to reaching your full potential.

Both physical and mental fitness are essential to your healthy well-being and involve focusing on and regularly orienting the body, mind, and spirit. Fitness of your mind is the opposite of physically sweating and pushing; it means slowing down and relaxing. A mental workout is quieting yourself, allowing you to identify thoughts and reactions to restructure them. That is the focus of this book.

Unlike exercise for the body, exercise for the mind is "the no-sweat way to sanity!" Instead of running, you relax; instead of breathing hard, you breathe rhythmically; instead of a racing heart, your heart beats softly, and so it goes. You get the idea. I think you will like it.

I have changed little in this new edition of *The Up Side of Being Down* besides the subtitle, minor restructuring and rewording, and shortening the chapters to accommodate our modern inclination to read smaller chunks of information. It was first published in the year 2001 and was used in seminars and group settings throughout the late 80s and 90s, from which the stories are drawn.

I also want to encourage you to use a notebook or journal to write down your insights and your responses to the reflection questions at the end of each chapter. The writing and journaling process adds greatly to our self-awareness.

Please look at www.mindfitnessbooks.com for more information and to make personal contact with me. Thank you for being interested in creating more peace within yourself, your families, and your communities. Welcome to learning how to use your mind to move to *The Up Side of Being Down!*

All the best thinking to you,

Joy L. Watson

Introduction

MILLIONS OF PEOPLE are trapped in a downward spiral of depression, anger, bitterness, and reactivity. Personal negativity has grown to such proportions it can now be considered an attitudinal addiction. Since cognition and attitude have become widely recognized as critical factors underlying health, this pervasive negativity undermines our personal and collective health. Lives are cut short, careers are stunted, and relationships wither because of negativity.

But there is an upside to the down attitude trap. Using the right tools allows you to find a way out and experience more vitality and happiness than you thought possible.

The Up Side of Being Down is a simple guide for healing personal negativity. It looks at a painful condition that has become as pervasive as Prozac and as insidious as toxic waste. The recommendations in this book will help you identify, accept, and heal dysfunctional attitudinal conditions using a self-guided approach called Mind Fitness.

Mind Fitness, like physical fitness, is a lifestyle that leads to better health and greater fulfillment. Instead of barbells and running shoes, Mind Fitness applies the tools of relaxation, proactive reflection, and whole-brain learning to create mental and emotional fitness that promotes lasting joy and well-being.

This approach embraces the principles of attitudinal healing, offering solutions for the problems of human health and well-being. The challenge of facing our negativity—both personally and collectively—plays a large part in the beginning of this new millennium. Mind Fitness is a timely and far-reaching mental health approach to help us do just that.

PART 1

Who, Me?

Identification and Acceptance

Chapter 1

Here We Go...

"My life looks great on paper. I have a wonderful family, a fine job, and good health. I should be happy, but much of the time, I feel depressed and out of control. Something is always wrong—at home or at work. Lately, life seems to be one irritation after another, something to be gotten through rather than enjoyed."

THIS THIRTY-FIVE-YEAR-OLD LEGAL secretary and mother of two teens speaks for millions of men and women. Their lives are basically good; their jobs are good. They love the people around them. They look just fine from the outside, but they're not as happy, satisfied, or at peace as they would like. They feel something is wrong and are not quite sure what it is.

They may experience waves of cynicism or pessimism sweeping over them "for no good reason." They may withdraw or lash out and say things they wish they hadn't said. They feel stressed and frustrated. There is an inconsistency in their responses. They feel out of balance. They are unduly hard on themselves, expecting more perfection. They don't trust themselves or believe that they have the power to shape their lives. They often feel defeated even before they begin. Sound familiar?

This cycle of negative feelings in all its many forms—fear, depression, anxiety, being overwhelmed, defeated, anger, pessimism, powerlessness, or anything that consistently prevents people from enjoying life——tends to feed on itself. It can be so subtle that we hardly recognize it, so insidious that we begin thinking it's just how we are. It takes so many different forms that it's difficult to pinpoint the problem exactly. Sometimes, we wonder, "Is there really a problem, or is this the way life is?" We just aren't sure. It's like having a persistent infection, a constant irritation that keeps us from feeling energetic, enthusiastic, and at peace with ourselves. We don't know what to do about it. We don't even know what to *call* the problem.

This book names Personal Negativity as a
mental health and attitudinal "Dis-Ease."

It offers specific behavioral learning solutions to reverse the cycle of painful and debilitating feelings often associated with an illness. The healing of a predominantly negative slant on life occurs as we learn to use our conscious minds constructively, appreciate ourselves and others more, and take control of our future attitudes and actions.

Here are some of the truths we've identified about personal forms of negative thinking:

- They may begin early in life.
- People often develop reactionary habits during their teen years, shaping personality and thinking patterns.
- They are a learned pattern of fearful perceptions and reactive thoughts and behaviors that feed and build on themselves, growing into an overall life attitude of anger, emotional defense, and protection.
- Because so many situations and people are seen through "gray-colored glasses," this condition drains energy and robs us of pleasure and happiness.
- Attitudes are contagious and pervasive, affecting others' perceptions and responses. An overall defensive, unpredictable, and reactionary attitude contaminates the social climate.
- The Up Side of this unhappy situation is that we can reverse and heal personal negativity with straightforward, powerful techniques that have proven effective in athletics, business, education, and health.

4

- We can learn to build increasingly satisfying attitudes, achieve goals, tap creative potential, and become happier, healthier, and more productive people.

The approach is Mind Fitness. It is a mental health training approach—a conscious way of thinking about how you want to live your life—with daily mental adjustments that do for the mind and heart what physical exercise does for the body. Mind Fitness work is entirely internal, invisible, and subjective.

We are the only ones who know our attitudes and what we value in life. We are the only ones who can direct our reactions, attitudes, and thinking.

Over the past twenty years, we have discovered that optimal performance in any field incorporates three basic skills: *relaxation, visualization, and affirmation.* These are the cornerstones of Mind Fitness practice training. Until now, many of us may have unknowingly used these three powerful mental tools to our detriment. Mind Fitness gives us a rationale and structure to use these skills to gain control of our attitudes, behaviors, and life directions.

This mental-focusing approach has three main components and is designed to enhance the quality of our personal and professional lives. It is a gentle but deliberate shift in perception——away from the habits of anger, defeat, and pessimism towards learning habits of fulfillment, productivity, satisfaction, and internal balance.

Healing personal negativity also means:

- **Nurturing,** first and foremost, a warmer, more confident, and generous relationship with ourselves.
- **Enhancing** the depth and quality of our relationships with loved ones, friends, and coworkers.
- **Enjoying** clearer direction and accomplishment in our work, community, and creative lives.
- **Living** more optimally in health, relationships, finances, and personal expressions of success.

This book defines negativity as "to see without love," meaning to see the limitations and impossibilities first. Healing is "to see with love," pointing to the potential possibilities.

The essence of Mind Fitness is the deliberate choice to do something regularly to enhance our mind's orientation and, therefore, our life direction.

Jerry Jampolsky, MD, founder of the Center for Attitudinal Healing, is a pioneer in this shift of thinking. He speaks about being a "love finder" rather than a "fault finder.' This simple difference is what attitudinal psychology is all about.

Personal Down-Sided negativity patterns are ways of thinking we have *learned* and repeatedly practiced; therefore, if we choose, we can learn new patterns with attitudes and behaviors that work *for* us rather than against us. We are not stuck in old patterns. We are learnable! This is the good news, the Up Side.

Let's look at attitudes for a moment. Attitudes are different from moods. Moods are feelings and can be like sunlight on a wall. They move around, change shapes frequently, bounce off various objects in different ways, and assume many different patterns in a day. A stream of sunlight may exist right alongside the darkest shadow.

In contrast, attitudes are not as quickly changeable as moods. They are steadier, more like the sun itself. Our attitudes reflect our baseline emotions—"where we live"—within ourselves. They are our base orientation, our predominant way of thinking. They determine whether we are open, welcoming, optimistic people who feel whole within ourselves and view life as a challenge and opportunity or people whose habitual negative thinking and attitudes make life seem like an obstacle course.

We are in charge of what our attitudes and thinking will be. We may have developed habitual attitudes early in life, but they can be changed to reflect what we want now. This flexibility—this ability to move from external to internal choices—lets us heal personal negativity and determine how we want to be in the world. We will have to overcome some early patterning and habits of thought, but developing new, more loving, and expansive thinking habits is possible for everyone.

It boils down to this:
1. Attitudinal thinking results from our personal, social, and cultural backgrounds and beliefs.
2. Our attitudes influence our moods and how we perceive and approach life.
3. We have the power to choose what our basic attitudes will be.

We can learn new ways of thinking based on choice, responsibility, and self-determination, oriented towards love and even happiness rather than on childhood helplessness, defensive anger, or fear.

When we start our personal Mind Fitness training, we consciously choose to take some control of our lives by putting ourselves into training that will result in our release from a condition that has been sapping our strength and energy for a long time. It is a choice for love, health, happiness, and developing our creativity and richest potential in all fields of endeavor.

Is that an ideal? Yes and no. It is a clear personal choice to actively learn to live a life designed around dynamic love and mental optimism.

Reflections

Ask yourself if you might be ready to make that clear personal choice for yourself to actively learn to live a life designed around dynamic love and mental optimism? If so, write in your journal: YES, I AM READY!

Chapter 2

What to Do?
Mind Fitness

MIND FITNESS ENCOURAGES the conscious use of our mind and spirit to heal negative thinking and replace it with more positive, creative, and enjoyable ways of relating to ourselves, one another, and our world. This is no add-on or extra; a regular mental health practice is integral to our ability to function successfully in our world.

As a framework for daily mental exercise and care, the practice of Mind Fitness leads to optimal health, creativity, and performance. Daily mental care does for the mind what physical fitness does for the body and helps promote excellence by exercising mental attitudes with creative images and self-spoken directed words.

"We become what we imagine" is our operating premise. The regular practice of Mind Fitness calls on the mind's most incredible untapped resource—the creative imagination—to form positive attitudes and then turn those attitudes into constructive action. Using the same core skills that peak performers use, we focus the mind, the will, and the imagination like a beam of light to help create the inner and outer realities we choose. By practicing our Mind Fitness program, we consciously use three powerful tools—relaxation, visualization, and affirmation—in our designed self-development and growth program.

Exercise for the Mind

We are just now beginning to know that, just as our bodies need proper nutrition and exercise, our minds and souls must also be fed, nurtured, and exercised with positive images and ideas to be healthy and peaceful. If we don't provide for and exercise our minds and bodies properly, we experience deficiencies. For the body, the deficiency may be anemia or lack of muscle tone; for the mind, the deficiency may be chronic low energy, abusive anger, lack of self-esteem, or other forms of negativity.

We can view our attitudes as muscles to be toned, stretched, and made more robust. If we don't flex those thinking muscles, we'll likely stay mired in our old habits of fear and negativity. A few decades ago, we didn't know it was necessary to exercise our bodies. There was a time when we didn't even know we should brush our teeth! We're now making the same discoveries about our minds and understanding that humans need a regular program of inner exercise and nourishment to stay healthy, positive, and pointed in the directions we ideally want to go.

As a society, we are increasingly realizing that "exercise"
for the mind is as essential for our health and
well-being as exercise for the body.

As we come to this realization, we are expanding our thinking about health. This book aims to present this developing concept within the Western world in terms that are direct and meaningful in our high-stress culture—thus, the words "Fitness" and "Dis-Ease." Negativity is not a disease or an illness in the same ways as a virus or a cold is. Instead, negativity creates feelings within us of disgruntled, disappointed, annoyed, stressed, angry, and irritated, making us uneasy and growling. We are in various states of non-alignment, discomfort, and "Dis-Ease." We are not calm, relaxed, or upbeat. We do not perceive the world accurately or function optimally. It is not a happy mental place to be.

There is something we can begin to do about this state of distress and Dis-Ease. We as a society have already accepted, intellectually, the need for regular physical fitness to support ourselves physically. The next step in our growth is to accept the need to engage in a regular time of Mind Fitness to support ourselves cognitively. Part of this daily mental care orientation is taking time out regularly to care for our minds in much the same way we care for our bodies. Without "exercising" through alert relaxation combined with positive images and ideas, our minds are inclined to atrophy into negative or passive states, just as our muscles atrophy when not used. During our Mind Fitness time, we "pump images" in much the same way that some people "pump iron."

Time-Out Sessions for Yourself

Time out provides a time for disconnecting. It is a few minutes to relax with awareness of our stressed-out, overworked minds, integrating and balancing them with our bodies, bringing both to a place of receptivity. We aren't going to sleep here! We are awake and mindful of our present moments. It is a time conducive to listening to our intuitive natures and understanding subtle points within the whole. A balanced mental state leads us in the right direction.

Just as saying a prayer helps us imagine positive images, by saying affirming words, we pump directive thoughts precisely to move ourselves in the direction we want. We create a *personalized* program of daily mental focus and exercise. One month, the focus may be on a health need; another month may be a professional or personal direction or a desired personality trait.

This quiet inner time is only part of the program. The Mind Fitness orientation involves a constant awareness that we are consciously growing and changing ourselves from within and altering our perceptions to live more creatively, contribute more to others, and learn to enjoy life more fully. We accept that we are evolving and need not be so afraid of changing our attitudes and actions as we learn more about ourselves and our world and how to care for both.

We can do Mind Lifts—short mental exercises in the form of constructive self-talk or reflective questions we ask ourselves—during the day. As we drive across town, wait in line at the market, or prepare for a big exam, business meeting, or social date, we can take a few seconds or minutes to remind ourselves how we want to feel and what we want to accomplish. We can remind ourselves of our values and how we want to interact or perform. We are taking control of our thoughts rather than letting fears and anger control them.

Mind Fitness, like physical fitness, is an empowering
program for our health and mental well-being.

It stems from the decision to move forward; we are choosing to change, grow, and embrace regular mental care as a framework to focus and accomplish our goals. We are taking more responsibility for our thoughts, actions, and lives.

Story: Adele always told people, "I don't do sports." She always refused when people asked her to go skiing, play tennis, or even go along on bicycle trips. As she began to examine this point of view about herself, she remembered something that had happened when she was in kindergarten. She and some other children were throwing a ball around. The teacher laughed at her, calling her "uncoordinated." Rather than repeat that embarrassing moment, Adele just stopped participating in games and started saying, "I don't do sports. I am too uncoordinated."

Soon, that point of view had become a reality as a personal constriction, a mental "dis-ability," holding her back from her full potential. She believed she was too uncoordinated to play sports, and she had never stopped to tell herself anything differently. When Adele started a self-development program, she thought about whether or not she wanted to continue that behavior and decided it was limiting her. She knew she might never become a great athlete, but she realized there were probably some physical activities—bicycling and jogging, for instance—that she could do and would enjoy.

Adele's Mind Fitness program included visualizing and affirming her ability to do and have fun with those things. She imagined herself doing different activities until she felt comfortable trying one.

To her surprise, she found that the sport she decided to take up was tennis—not only for the sociability and the vigorous exercise but because her visualizations had shown her that she was a competitive person. The thrill of winning was important to her and would hold her interest.

Armed with her newly focused direction and some courage, Adele signed up for a women's beginner class at the local tennis courts. She discovered that she loves the feel and sound of the ball hitting her racket, and her coordination is just as good as her classmates'. In the past two years, Adele has been regularly playing other women at her level—and, to her delight, she has become a pretty good tennis player.

Reflections

Take three to five deep breaths, inhaling through the nose and exhaling slowly through the mouth.

Experience taking a few moments of Time Out for yourself. No pressure, just a moment of quiet.

How does that feel to you?

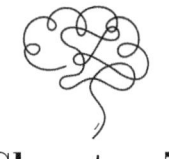

Chapter 3

Every Day?
Regular Mental Quiet

REGULAR MENTAL QUIETING teaches us how to use the mind to bridge our inner knowing—our intuition and true desires—and our capacity to act in the world. We can use the powers of the calm, focused mind, emotions, and imagination to shift from negative to positive attitudes and from others' ideas of what we should be and do to our *own* ideas of what we want to be and do.

The "dream first, act second" model turns out to be an accurate learning model for human change.
As a learning technology, Mind Fitness guides us to unlearn old habits and learn new ones using specific thinking processes. We open up and sharpen our minds, enhancing the quality of our personal and professional lives.

Strong mental fitness creates better overall mental health, supporting all areas of life: career, relationship, creativity, sports, learning, health, hobbies, finance, etc. When we learn to think in focused ways, we see the results in our positive approach to each day, our ability to handle stress, our energy level, our self-esteem, our sense of enjoyment and accomplishment in the quality of our relationships, and the generosity of spirit in which we hold ourselves and others.

Mind Fitness sessions help us learn to:
- **Break the cycle** of negative attitudes by recognizing and releasing those old habits, patterns, attitudes, and automatic reactions.
- **Identify new goals** that are important to us—and move toward them.
- **Turn new, positive habits** of thought into constructive actions that increase our well-being and satisfaction so we are happier and can fulfill more of our potential.
- **Make the transition** from fear and helplessness to active love and self-determination in our lives.
- **Shift the focus** from psychological pain and emotional survival to love of self, generosity of spirit, and compassion for others.
- **Build a solid base** of optimistic belief in ourselves from which to approach our lives and relationships with dynamic love.

Proactive Reflection

The inner-quieting practice makes us aware of our thoughts and guides us to where we want to go. We focus on and identify personally destructive attitudes and thinking, accept them, and replace them with powerful mental images of:
- How we want to feel and act.
- What we want our lives to be, inside and out.
- What we want to contribute and accomplish.
- How to reach those goals.

Taking time out for proactive personal reflection on our behalf combines healing with empowerment and lets us actively take charge of our lives.

We consciously reflect on the kinds of perceptions and attitudes that we want to dominate our lives and then translate those values into meaningful goals and actions. We actively use the mind to bridge our inner knowing, our soul's journey, and our daily lives in the outer world. We take time to think about who and what we are, balance our emotions, and set our energies in the direction we want to develop. We don't solve all our problems immediately, but over time, we approach them with growing consciousness and confidence.

16

The practice of inner quiet stimulates us to take charge of our lives in two ways: We clarify our desire to be a value-centered person, interested in optimal health and well-being, and we take responsibility for whether or not we become that person. We have a structure in which to heal—to connect with our inner strength and wisdom, to confront our fears gently, and to affirm our full potential. Using Mind Fitness principles, we identify our goals, visualize and affirm how to reach them, and confidently set out on that path.

Add-On Thinking

Daily mental care and exercise represent an evolution in how we think about life and ourselves. It is part of a natural progression toward higher levels of thinking and interaction that enhance our lives.

This evolution in thought is what I call Add-On Thinking. Add-On Thinking enables us to expand our thinking, produce more change, and have better life results at no extra cost. We are encouraged to operate at levels we might have thought were beyond us.

In a simplified view, Add-On Thinking means calling on the brain's intuitive, image-oriented functions to enhance the logical, language-oriented functions. We combine the creative and analytical brain functions. We can think of it as having the two halves of the brain work together in integrated and synergistic ways, making the whole more significant than the sum of its parts.

In our educational system, most of us have been taught to use the "logical" brain—the "slice, dice, and shuffle" method of thinking. We learn and practice logical analysis, systematic reduction, and rational deduction, making our thinking more precise each time. This is the scientific approach, which is very important to learn. We keep cutting up the hard facts in different ways and shuffling them into different combinations, but in order to develop new ideas and perspectives, we need to also use new "imaginary" thinking. This is also called "what if?" thinking.

The Mind Fitness thinking process draws on these analytical skills—and adds on the creative, synthesizing skills to include imaging and patterning. This is an integrative approach. It teaches "possibility thinking," using the imagination almost as a sixth sense to improve our health and performance in any activity. Taking the time to reflect proactively, we become more aware of who we are—our shadows and our values—and how we interact with the rest of the world.

Both imaginative and analytical thinking are
essential if we want to be and do our best.

They are meant to *complement* one another, not *compete* with one another. The goal is to be grounded in the "real world" and foster creativity and personal development.

Because we are more accustomed to using the analytical function, we may have to put more emphasis at first on learning about and working with intuitive, imaginative abilities. These are skills that *can* be fostered with some attention on our part. We may have hesitated to call on this vital resource in our pragmatic world, and some of us have reached the point where we need to remember our imaginative faculties and what they can do for us. This is learnable.

When I look back, I realize I had a moment of Add-On Thinking when I changed my mind about my then- 16-year-old daughter having a car to drive around town. I had entered a deep quiet time, following my breathing for about a half an hour. I wasn't thinking about this particular situation, but suddenly, a thought came to mind that if my daughter was not driving herself, then she would be driven around by other young people. I realized that I trusted her to drive more than I trusted other new unknown drivers. I got the image of her driving happily and safely. In a flash, and to my shock, I experienced a complete reversal in my thinking when I allowed a deeper intuitive sense to arise from the quiet. It came from a totally new perspective and added on a totally new realization within me. Needless to say, she was delighted!

As we learn to recognize and use both powerful components of our minds, we become increasingly fulfilled and actualized. We become capable of more significant concepts and perceptions, aware of more subtleties and emerging patterns. We work closer to our potential and experience more of life because we enjoy greater insight. We see things in different ways. We think of things we haven't thought of before. New ideas spring to mind. It's as if we've suddenly noticed a secret panel in a familiar room, even though it has been there all along.

Add-On Thinking acts like a synthesizing process.
It takes us to a whole new level of thought, a skill
nurturing creativity and innovation.

Reflections

Add-On Thinking is about envisioning possibilities by using our imaginations. Sit quietly for some time, breathing with awareness, relaxing your body and thinking mind.

Can you imagine one part of your life offering you a fuller possibility of satisfaction and joy? How might you shift into what is called Add-On Thinking, expanding a boundary into a new possible intention or goal for yourself?

Is it too early for you to put that into words? If not, write a short sentence about your expanding thought.

Chapter 4

Benefits?
Generosity of Spirit...

As with physical fitness, people describe many benefits when incorporating a Mind Fitness orientation into their lives. Their relationships get better, they experience more satisfaction (and usually more success) in their work, they feel better physically and have more energy, they often perform better in sports and competitions, and they generally get more involved in life and have more fun. People feel more in balance and assured of their direction.

The most far-reaching benefit many experience is a feeling that comes from deep within of kindness and generosity toward ourselves and others. Our fears are lessened as we get to know ourselves better. As we experience a daily time to relax and be mentally quiet, we are more willing to forgive and accept. We are emotionally in balance more often. No, we are not perfect! But we work to expand our conscious awareness and increasingly understand that we all have both faults and magnificent qualities. This is borne out in our behaviors toward others, which tend to grow more compassionate and empathetic. We are less emotionally reactive.

As we quiet each day, we are less likely to condemn and more likely to embrace others respectfully and lovingly.
With its inherent generosity of spirit and compassion, this enhanced ability to love extends to other people, our families and communities,

and ourselves. The gentler we are with ourselves—the more we love ourselves—the more we can love others. And the more we love others, the more we can love ourselves. It becomes a dynamic upward spiral. The love and understanding we feel for ourselves and others become an additional fuel that fires our success in work, play, and every area of life.

Love as an optimistic way of thinking is a learned behavior. It means working through personal fears and opening up to others with some degree of trust. People with difficulty relaxing and opening up can learn to enjoy the most pleasurable human emotions more frequently.

Story: Richard is an insurance broker who joined one of our groups. When he shared that he had trouble opening up to people and felt overcome with shyness, no one doubted him for a minute. He sat in a completely closed posture—arms and legs crossed, chin on chest, eyes glued to the floor. At the same time, it was evident that he desperately wanted more friendship and socializing in his life.

Richard opened up gradually during the meetings as he practiced various Mind Fitness exercises. He felt safe enough to extend himself to the other group members and let in their support and friendship. It didn't happen overnight or even over the first month, but Richard took steps to overcome his shyness and fear of people. At last report, he surprised himself and others with his newfound ability to be present with them, to open up and share, to laugh and relax, and to love others—as well as himself.

Learning to love ourselves is at the core of Mind Fitness. Don't let the word "love" scare you off. It is challenging to let ourselves be creative, healthy, and peaceful, leading what we so casually term "a happy life," if we don't love and accept ourselves. Positive, supportive energy moves in a spiral cycle, touching us as it touches others. It is an attitude and a perceptual ground of being through which we view life in general.

Love means being willing to see the best and
pardon the worst in ourselves and others.

We enter into a radical trust as we open ourselves to each other, unconditionally believing that things eventually turn out for the best.

Self-love is an acquired or learned skill. Most of us are not brought up to love ourselves. The word "love" is often considered inappropriate and too soft to be effective in much of the business, academic, and scientific worlds. We're raised to behave and not be arrogant or "full of ourselves."

The Mind Fitness philosophy gets around the harshness of this type of upbringing by giving us a structure in which we are supposed to be kind and gentle with ourselves, in which listening to our inner quiet is *necessary work*. It provides us with a rational excuse to be generous with ourselves.

A daily time of quiet and inner focus helps us learn to approach the world not from infancy's frantic helplessness, fear, and anger but from a caring adult's loving acceptance, self-determination, and generosity.

Healing

Healing means recognizing and accepting our negative emotional and thinking patterns and breaking these unwanted cycles as we focus on learning to see with expanded possibilities. The most challenging step is initially admitting to ourselves that we are more negative in attitude and perceptions than we want to be. Secondly, we want to grow into a more open and optimistic person. In the pages ahead, we will learn how to help ourselves heal. In order to start moving in that direction, it may be helpful to look at healthy attitudes to orient us.

Here are some of the healthy attitudes and behaviors that help us break cycles of personal negativity:

- Our initial reactions to new people and things are welcoming and optimistic. We are open to the possibility that they will be a force for good in our lives.
- We value a sense of humor. We can laugh at ourselves and can easily have fun.
- We are intimate and share ourselves fully without hiding behind cynicism, anger, depression, or criticism.
- We can admit to some negative feelings, knowing that they represent only a part of our experience—not all.
- We don't have to worry about whether or not we are happy.
- We do what feels suitable for us. We trust our intuition.

- We meet each day with self-confidence and favorable expectations rather than a gnawing dread.
- We have compassion for others. We can give freely without feeling that we are making a sacrifice. We want to support others in doing their best. We can admire others because we don't fear that we lose if they win.
- We feel good, worthy, and in control enough to handle the tasks before us.
- We let ideas of who we are and what we want to do emerge from within ourselves rather than having them dictated by external forces.
- We maintain a level of self-discipline that makes us feel good about ourselves. We are focused and have clear priorities.
- We feel a balance among the many aspects of our lives.

Are we all of those wonderful things at all times? I doubt it, but knowing some signposts helps us chart our path.

Reflections

Thoughtfully reread the bulleted list of above.

Pick out one or two healthy attitudes and behaviors that you would like to see expand into greater possibilities in your life.

I picked out #2 on the list about adding humor and laughing more with myself.

What are yours?

Chapter 5

Picture This!
We Become What We Image

RECENT RESEARCH SHOWS powerful connections between the mind and body, attitudes and actions, and what we think and do. It is becoming common knowledge that performance can be improved by first entering an alert, relaxed state and then visualizing and experiencing the activity mentally, precisely as we would like to do it. Mental rehearsal and visualization principles have been used extensively for peak performance in sports; now, they are used by professionals in business, education, medicine, and health.

More than ever before, we have come to appreciate that "thoughts are things." This ability to create self-fulfilling prophecies in our minds and to affect reality with mental images is how personal negative thinking habits come into being—and how they are healed.

Thoughts Are Things

The idea that skills can be honed, attitudes enhanced, and performance improved by seeing the desired results in the mind's eye is not new. Optimal performers in all fields have long used visualization, and its effectiveness in sports has been evident for some time.

What is new in the past twenty years is that the scientific community has been testing and studying this phenomenon called the neurophysiology of learning. Scientists have agreed that it is a powerful method of changing and improving mental and physical conditions.

Increasingly, medical and educational research shows thoughts carry information that affects and creates overall physical health and peak performance.

Dr. Willis Harmon, past president of the Institute of Noetic Sciences, wrote, *"One of the most far-reaching of the findings related to consciousness has been dubbed the 'self-fulfilling prophecy.' More precisely, it is our beliefs, conscious and unconscious, that create the future in ways more subtle and more powerful than we ordinarily take into account."*

In his introduction to Norman Cousins' *Anatomy of an Illness*, Rene Dubos wrote, *"Cousins repeatedly states that the mental attitudes of patients have a lot to do with the course of their disease and illustrates this theme with examples taken from clinical material. It is common knowledge, of course, that the mind influences the body and vice versa . . ."*

At well-respected institutions such as the Menninger Clinic, the Simonton Clinic, UCLA, Stanford University, and Harvard Medical School, doctors and researchers are showing that we can gain mastery over physiological functions through mental imagery, relaxation, meditation, visualization, and affirmation. These techniques have proven effective in normalizing heart rates, reducing stress, and decreasing pain in burn units, and may even be responsible for some unexplained remissions in cancer.

Peak Performers

People who want to be the best in their fields have not waited for research to validate methods they knew worked. Some of the most accomplished people in the world use the principles of relaxation, visualization, and meditation to achieve their optimal performance:

Sports and Education: Early pioneering leaders in the constructive use of focused thinking include such long-time great athletes as Masters golfer Jack Nicklaus, tennis champion Stan Smith, and seven-time American League Batting champion Rod Carew; and Olympic gold medalists such as skier Jean-Claude Killy, diver Greg Louganis, and swimmer Janet Evans. These greats set the stage for inner mind training.

In sports, visualization is often called mental rehearsal and is a key aspect of sports psychology.

Education: Educators call these same techniques accelerated learning; they are applying skills that have been used for years in teaching. Mental seeing and hearing is a skill that, once learned, can be applied to many areas of learning. This approach is now a part of the learning environment in many "can-do" classrooms. In this course of study, students learn how to imagine their success in school, on the playing field, and in their daily lives.

Business and Medicine: Corporations now acknowledge the value of creative intuition and logical analysis, increasingly using visualization to plan and achieve individual and corporate goals. This interest is evidenced by the considerable growth of corporate seminars to develop peak performance and leadership skills in management. Increasingly, these seminars emphasize visual communication, including the use of imagination, mental rehearsal, and iconic symbols. It's all part of a corporate effort to increase creative problem-solving.

In medicine, "lifestyle diseases" refers to conditions that do not come from bacteria or viruses but from continual life stresses that affect both body and mind. Pioneers in biofeedback and cardiology are demonstrating astounding relationships between the mind's thoughts and the body's cardiovascular and immune systems. Mental imagery has also proven helpful in dealing with some cancers, in childbirth, in reducing pain in burn clinics, and in promoting overall physical health. In medicine, Mind Fitness techniques are usually called guided imagery, stress reduction, or wellness techniques.

The optimal performance-enhancing skills common to all these fields are relaxation, visualization, and affirmation. Each program encourages optimal mental and physical performance through mental focusing—the conscious choice of and concentration on specific thoughts.

Proactive reflection encourages the individual to take the time and responsibility to determine the desired outcome.

These principles can be applied to any endeavor. A jogger uses the same mental focusing skills to improve his running that a cancer patient uses to promote her body's well-being; an executive looking for a creative solution uses the same techniques as a student studying for an exam.

Reflections

Now that you know how successful the simple steps of relaxing, visualizing a desired sequence of actions, and affirming your goal in words can be, it is time to give that a try.

Take a few breaths as you settle quietly and use your imagination to create your own personal "self-fulfilling prophecy."

This should be something you would like to see develop in your life, whether it be expansion of a personal characteristic, development of a skill, or relief from a medical issue.

Remember, your "self-fulfilling prophecy" is recharged through your mental focus and conscious concentration on this specific thought.

Make this your Mind Lift. Repeat it in your mind often as if you are an athlete practicing shooting baskets. Breathe, see, and say as you live your prophecy into possibility.

Chapter 6

How About a Map? Coping to Creating

W<small>HETHER OR NOT</small> we know it, we have often worked against ourselves. We have imagined and visualized things that make us angry, fearful, or anxious. We don't realize that when we daydream and mentally roll something over, we are making it more real to us by ingraining it in our brains.

We often imagine something and then discover some of these thoughts manifest in reality. If there doesn't seem to be a pattern to this manifestation, it is because there probably hasn't been much clarity in our visualizations. We are not taught to sit down and figure out what we want in life, much less to incorporate visual imagery and inner thinking to help achieve our goals. More importantly, we are not warned that if we sit around brooding, lost in negative thoughts, or pondering resentments, we create our own negativity.

Given the lack of information we've received and not knowing the power of intuition and visualization, it's astonishing how well most of us have done! When we understand the power of visual imagery as a critical, productive mind tool, we can begin to make our own choices and take an active role in what happens in our lives.

What We Can Do About It Now

All this means is that we have some control of our destinies. We begin by becoming aware of our personal learned patterns and triggers. What we have learned, we can unlearn. We have taught ourselves one thing: we can teach ourselves something else.

Our old negative viewpoints have been formed from feelings of helplessness, fear, and anger. We can use the same mental techniques to reshape those old viewpoints and shift our thinking so that our base of operation becomes love, self-determination, and growth. We can begin to *choose* how we use these powerful tools of mental focusing. We are no longer helpless. It takes courage to accept our shadow, but once we do, we can teach ourselves to deal with the world as loving, accepting, creative adults.

Old patterns can be altered with thinking skills, and thinking skills can be learned. Thoughts create attitudes and actions; we can learn to guide and amplify them. To change our lives, we must discover which ideas have us perceive our life negatively and consciously focus on refocusing those thoughts. The ability to do this through daily mental care allows us to create a shift to concentrate on optimal personal development.

Moving from Coping to Creating

I first encountered this idea of psychological and spiritual evolution in the works of Dr. Abraham Maslow. This evolution isn't physical; we don't need to grow a new kind of ear or eye to survive. We need a change in consciousness, a quantum leap in how we perceive ourselves and our world. To make this leap, we must tap abilities and potentials that we have ignored or not developed until now. Mind Fitness, as an attitude-to-action approach to inner and outer peace, is designed to help us make such a leap in consciousness, personally and as a society.

Dr. Maslow's theory of personal development and human needs suggests that we move naturally from living life at the level of *coping*—just barely able to satisfy our physical and psychological needs—to living at the level of creating, where we fulfill our potential and become self-actualized.

When I first read Dr. Maslow's book *Toward a Psychology of Being* in my undergraduate days, I felt as if I had been given a road map to how I wanted to develop and live my life. A light bulb went off in my head, and I knew my path. Maslow described a human "hierarchy of needs," a progression from one level to the next. A shortened version goes like this:

1. **Physical Survival.** We are concerned about food, shelter, clothing, and physical safety at this level. Most of our energy goes into physical survival. This level is characterized by fear and desperation, and our thinking tends to be survival oriented. Before moving on to the next level, we must establish some degree of physical security, a base of safety in which our bodily survival is not threatened.

2. **Emotional Safety and Self-Worth.** The next level is psychological and includes friendship, self-esteem, and winning respect from others. Maslow's research showed that when we do not feel competent or do not feel respected for who we are and what we do, our self-worth comes into doubt, and we feel unsafe. This psychological deprivation leads to anger, hostility, and harsh judgment of others. When we can't accept others, we can't accept ourselves, making it even more difficult to accept others. It becomes a downward cycle. We are afraid not for our physical safety but for our emotional security and self-worth—still, we are living in fear. Before moving on, we must satisfy our needs to feel worthwhile, loved, and respected by the people around us.

3. **Self-Actualization.** The first two levels involve physical and psychological security. This third level moves us into a more self-fulfilling mindset, where we begin to satisfy our self-expression and creativity needs. This is the area of optimal and peak performance. It might be in the arts, sports, higher learning, or some other field, but this is the level at which we see extraordinary achievements and thriving people. Maslow calls these people "self-actualized." Psychologist Dr. Carl Rogers used the term "fully functioning human." These people no longer live out of a sense of deficiency or scarcity; instead,

they feel an expansion, a sense of self-worth and confidence that makes more room for achievement and creativity. These self-actualized people live optimally and are capable of remarkable achievements and success.

Mind Fitness provides a framework to teach people how to become self-actualized and live at this fully developed, optimal level.

According to Dr. Maslow, self-actualized people tend to have deep connections with others and experience love not only for the people with whom they come in contact but for all the human race. There is a spiritual aspect to their lives with a strong sense of the interconnectedness to all life and a trust in their intuitive sense to guide them.

These are some of the other ways Maslow's work has described self-actualized people:

- They enjoy life in nearly all of its moments and aspects, whereas other people have only limited moments of enjoyment.
- They are spontaneous, creative, open to new experiences, and relatively unafraid of the unknown.
- They feel dominion in their lives and demonstrate healthy selfishness, which means they respect their activities and guard their time accordingly.
- Their work and play overlap and become equally absorbing and satisfying.
- Because of their substantial self-knowledge, self-acceptance, and the relative absence of fear, they are not hostile toward others.
- They are quick to love and be loved.

Reflections

This reflection is good to do after you settle in by taking a few deep breaths.

Let's take a look at Maslow's road map leading us to becoming self-actualized, fully functioning people.

Start with the physical-survival level, which most of us have relatively secured. Look around you and consciously name things that contribute to your physical survival in life. I do this by saying, "Thank you for my home, for my indoor plumbing and hot water. Thank you for my refrigerator and cabinets with food sitting in them. Thank you for water to drink that I don't have to haul. Thank you for my shoes, and boots to wear in the winter. Thank you for my closet offering me daily choices." You get the idea. I continue, naming and granting a moment of appreciation and stated gratitude for my good fortune in having my physical needs met.

Now reflect on your feelings of psychological safety and self-worth. This is not so concrete and can vary with time, situations, and people. Are you verbally or emotionally attacked often or chronically dissed by some people? Do you have groups and relationships that you belong to where you feel respected and liked? Is your work situation one where you feel a sense of achievement and self-worth?

Continue over a few weeks to really examine this more abstract level of your life and how your feelings of self interact with your daily life.

The next reflection is to think what it would feel like to live with a sense of interconnectedness to all life and live your own sense of purpose and fulfillment while going about your days with a feeling of trust and lightheartedness. If you have job you don't like, is there a way to make it more purposeful, more enjoyable? How can you change your thinking to make it meaningful?

Review the description of actualized people at the very end of this chapter and pick out one or two you want to focus on achieving. For me, it is the characteristic of work and play overlapping and becoming equally absorbing and satisfying. What is yours?

Chapter 7

Want to Try Love? Optimal Living

MIND **F**ITNESS **BRINGS** together two powerful concepts:

1. The concept of *daily mental care*—using the proven learning techniques of aware relaxation, mental imagery, and affirmations to influence our attitudes and our lives, and

2. The concept that *we evolve and grow* by continually upgrading the quality of our lives—moving from physical survival through emotional safety to self-actualization with its powerful energies for love, creativity, and fulfillment.

The practice of Mind Fitness quickens our path toward precisely where we want to be much the time on the hierarchy of needs. We can focus on developing the character and lives we want. The aware relaxation, visualization, and affirmation techniques take us beyond the physical and psychological realm into the spiritual realm, the realm of creativity and connection with the infinite. There, we experience on a deeper level the meaning of unlimited capacity to be whatever we want to be, with no boundaries or limits.

We may concentrate on peak performance in sports—improving our tennis game, running, or weightlifting. Our external goals may center on professional areas—self-improvement, a change of career, or being a better manager. We may want to concentrate on being excellent learners to master a new area of interest, or we may want to improve our health. We may want to focus on being better parents or spouses.

Optimizing one area of our lives always spills over into all other areas.

Living as loving and creative people is living life to the fullest. Mental well-being guides us *to choose* to optimize our lives rather than just waiting around to see whether or not it happens.

Love: The Bottom Line

As we continue our personal development, we all want to love and see ourselves and others with positive regard. The desire to love and be loved is even more fundamental than the initial helplessness with which we enter the world. It is truly our home base.

Expanding love and creativity are the focus of an actualizing life.

Inner mental and spiritual focus is a way of life that guides us to move consciously *out* of our long-standing habits and addictions of helplessness, fear, and anger *into* expressive lives built on a love of self and others. This focus embodies the willingness to strive towards the possibilities, the optimistic, and the positive—just as a plant reaches for the light.

This shift in thinking is the recognition that we, personally and collectively, are moving—quickly or slowly—out of pessimism and into optimism, out of anger and into self-expression. Love offers compassion; it expresses that we are all connected and that, on some level, we are all striving for harmony and continued development. There is a sense of gratitude that dwells within our hearts and minds.

Consciously Design Your Life

An essential part of practicing Mind Fitness is consciously designing your life around this kind of love. Dynamic love. Love that is constantly changing and growing as that mental attitude influences our lives.

Being a loving person is a skill to be cultivated and nurtured.

Because we're all human and subject to the pain, fear, and anger that become part of our makeup, we can't simply assume that love will just come to us without being called. We need to make known *our intention to love*—first and foremost to ourselves—and then we need to do something about it. As we become proactive for love, we focus on love as something we consciously create for and in our lives. Then, the healing process begins.

Writing a Gratitude List is one of the most well-publicized ways to start focusing on love. Reflect upon your daily experiences and write five things you are grateful for. These can be tiny moments, such as seeing a sunset, having the correct change for the bus, or hugging your child in a quick moment of sweetness. As we consciously start to appreciate the small things of life, our fear and anger begin to dissolve, controlling us less as they become more balanced within us emotionally. This first occurs on a personal level and then expands to our relationships, families, and the larger community.

Loving ourselves is at the very heart of vital mental health.
By entering into this philosophy and orientation of caring for ourselves and reshaping our lives, we have given ourselves a gift of kindness and self-determined power. We have begun to put our values at the center of our lives and sense our connection with something infinite—the spirit in all of us that allows us to go beyond what we thought we were.

Reflections

Start carrying around the idea of consciously creating your life around love.

In your journal, begin your gratitude list by writing down five things you are grateful for this very minute.

Take a deep breath as you smile, feeling how lucky you are to experience those things in your life.

Chapter 8

How Did It Start?
The Beginnings...Maybe

W E MAY HAVE become aware that we have a negative slant on the world and have consciously decided to work on a more positive and constructive life attitude. We have decided to work on learning how to use the untapped power of our imaginative minds and spirits to become active in creating love, inner peace, creativity, accomplishment, and increased happiness in our lives. We want to be proactive by developing new mental habits that contribute more to the world and simultaneously lead us to experience more joy, growth, pleasure, and satisfaction.

When we think like this, we've begun to opt for lives
about self-determination and possibilities
rather than limitations and barriers.

This is my thinking on how the Down Side may have begun. The way negative mental and emotional patterns get started is unique to each individual, but a common thread concerns our early feelings of the pain of helplessness. Initially, we experience harmony—the harmony of love and peace as we create and grow in the womb. All is tranquil and cared for in our world. Love and growth can be thought of as our home base.

Our birth brings many changes. The first thing that happens to us after birth is that we are deprived of a situation where all our needs have been met. In the womb, we float effortlessly in an environment designed to do nothing but support us. We have a steady flow of nutrition; temperature and waste removal are never problems.

Despite the best intentions, things quickly get unpleasant when we are born. Suddenly, our needs are *not* met automatically. We are entirely helpless. We must do something about it. Helplessness is the first after-birth experience we all share, becoming the foundation for most of our subsequent perceptions and understandings. It is an initial fact of life for everyone. Our original place of comfort and peace has been shattered. We are out in the big world now and depend on others for food, protection, cleanliness, and affection.

Helplessness quickly prompts feelings of fear.

We are vulnerable. If we are left alone, the chances are good that we won't survive. All young children fear being abandoned—and with good reason. Professionals tell us that one of the worst things we can do to a toddler is to pretend we'll leave her if she doesn't hurry. It reinforces this deep fear of being unable to care for herself by being threatened to be left behind by the people who *care* for her.

So we can't take care of ourselves, and the people who are supposed to care for us don't always do a perfect job. As babies, we were fed foods we didn't like, we didn't get changed as often as we wanted, we had our bottoms wiped in ways that were uncomfortable and may have hurt, we were made to do things we didn't want to do, and we were not allowed to do something we wanted to do. We may have been tossed in the air when we were scared, tickled past the point of fun, or played with while experiencing fear and frustration.

Many were outrightly abused physically and psychologically, intentionally or unintentionally. Emotional pain from early abuse or experiences is a marked factor in forming our thinking patterns. Pain affects everything: how we perceive our world and others and respond to situations. Only now are we, as a society, beginning to realize the psychological damage of many of the child-rearing practices we found acceptable in the past. Things are coming to light and seen as part of the taproot of negativity. The types of abuse and alienation that people suffer have a profound impact on our lives. Many adolescents and adults seek support groups to learn how to move past their fears and anger to live more trusting and peaceful lives.

Original Anger

We all have experienced the fears and frustrations of not being in charge of our lives, and many people have been abused by the people who had control over them. It may have looked different for each of us, but we all have experienced original anger by age five. Original anger is the anger we may have inside from early life experiences. After birth, we experience a degree of helplessness that often leads to fear and a wave of insidious anger. Once we recognize and accept our anger and adverse reactions, we often want to learn how to experience our home base of love.

As children, we grew up dwelling on these early fearful feelings, reacting to them, and all too often having them set the tone for our mental fantasy play. Thus, the fundamental attitudinal backdrop to our lives was formed. This is especially true if we suffered from physical or psychological abuse and other extreme forms of negativity.

Fantasy is an integral part of any child's play. This childhood mind-play is a powerful tool that can be used to our detriment or advantage. The versions of mind-play are endless and unique to each individual's life. We didn't have much wisdom in handling this potential tool when we were young and got little instruction. As a result, many of us used our mind-play in ways that later turned out to be limiting and self-destructive. We did not realize that our fantasy play could have such a potent effect on our lives or, more so, that it could crystallize into a lifelong habit of thinking. In comes the Down Side.

Most of us can remember how, as teens, we retreated to our rooms and continued a somewhat more sophisticated version of this imaging and fantasy play. We daydreamed for hours, fueled by all the emotions from not experiencing our home base of love: fear, anger, sadness, frustration. We saw ourselves as victims, even as martyrs. We developed coping mechanisms: resistance, toughness, whining, "getting even" in petty ways—whatever we thought could help us endure those difficult years.

41

If we felt accepted and in control of our lives, we probably used our imaginations more constructively and fantasized about being heroic, clever, successful, or artistic, or performing incredible athletic feats. We created a self-portrait and belief system during the many hours we spent in mental play. This set the tone for our attitudes as adults. During those years, we started developing the positive and negative filters through which we now view life. We were actively teaching ourselves a *learned* response to the people and events around us.

> *Our emotion-packed daydreams in early childhood*
> *and adolescence often set an attitudinal tone that*
> *affects everything we do and see as adults.*

If we concentrated on blaming others for our feelings of helplessness and anger—with feelings of "I can't," or "They're picking on me," or "Poor me," or "I always get the short end"—then we taught ourselves a predominant perception of the world: one filled with feelings of fear, bitterness, impatience, defeatism, and despair. Our governing theme became, "I never win; life is hard, and I am not in control." In contrast, if we spent time daydreaming constructively about our abilities, we would more likely emerge as adults who approach life with satisfaction, fulfillment, and self-confidence.

This may be how predominantly negative thinking patterns begin and grow during adolescence. We teach ourselves to approach life with varying degrees of positive or negative thinking—usually without any idea of what we are doing. As adults, these clusters of attitudes and behaviors are so much a part of us that we hardly know they are there. They form our primary thinking mode. We cannot change it until we recognize our patterns and their source.

- So, how do we recognize personal negativity in ourselves?
- What is it, exactly, that hurts?
- How can we refocus our perceptions?

Reflections

Think about your earlier life and adolescence.

Allow yourself to recall your earlier thinking patterns without judgment, only curiosity.

Chapter 9

Are You Unique?
Yep, Custom-Made

EVERYONE EXPERIENCES NEGATIVITY differently. **Can you recognize any of these feelings?**

- Insatiability: a sense that there is never enough (love, money, food, sunshine, cleanliness, beauty, and so on), a feeling of never being satisfied: "I want more!" or " The grass is always greener on the other side of the fence."
- Endless complaining and whining: feeling defeated and victimized by the world: "They didn't let me," or "They did it to me."
- Anger, irritation, a habit of springing into self-righteous judgments without warning or provocation: "You idiot! You did it all wrong. I could have done it better."
- Dark feelings of apathy or depression: "What's the use? Nothing will work anyway."
- Never being able to do or be enough: "I just wanted to . . ."
- Feeling pressured and overwhelmed: "I will never be able to do all of this," or "I am the only one who works this hard."
- Haunting fears and phobias that keep life from being expansive and fulfilling: "I don't know why, but I just can't do it. I am scared."

Definition: Negativity is an overriding feeling of resistance to every task and opportunity. Nothing seems easy—or if it is, it is made more difficult by being plagued with doubts, indecision, and unfavorable judgments. Negativity lacks positive qualities. Merriam-Webster dictionary lists synonyms for negative as disagreeable, hostility, withdrawal, pessimism, adversary, antagonistic, and unfriendly. Vocabulary.com simply says, "Negative means focused on what is bad or lacking." Collins Dictionary writes, "having the effect of diminishing, depriving, or denying." The Britannica lists negative as "expressing dislike or disapproval; showing or talking about the bad qualities of someone or something."

Commonly, the responsibility for feelings and life is placed on the *external*, with a negative, self-limiting twist. These feelings are self-imposed and subjective, often not in sync with worldly success. This syndrome of shadow emotions and behaviors manifests itself in as many ways as there are individuals who experience it, but most often in the form of beliefs and feelings that life is unfair—with a predominant reaction of helplessness, insecurity, defeatism, fear, and anger. Often, these feelings consume us without our conscious awareness.

> *None of us will ever be perfect,*
> *with a constant "up" slant on life.*

Even the most devoted monks have their down days. We cannot expect to "correct" *every* attitude that keeps life from being as full or happy as it might be. But to change any of these attitudes, it's essential to identify them. We must become aware of what we want to move away from while working to develop other qualities within ourselves. Then, we can plan active strategies to replace old attitudes with new ones, heal old hurts, and begin living more positively, and dare I use the word happier.

Protection and Survival

We didn't come into the world with automatic adverse reactions. My thinking is we learned these attitudes and behaviors as responses to our early environments, as means of surviving what we thought we could not in any other way. For the most part, we learned these behaviors *unconsciously.* We did what we felt we needed to do to protect ourselves successfully, and then we adopted those behaviors as a way of living—

again, without much thought. Twenty, forty, or sixty years later, we find ourselves using those same behaviors—whether or not they're relevant to anything in our lives now. They may have been effective, even necessary, back then. However, if we examine them today, we can see that they have become long-standing *habits* that we use primarily in response to varying degrees of stress. They do not lead us toward a happier, more fulfilled life; they stand in our way.

Story: When Stan examined his pattern of coming down with a cold or the flu whenever his wife had to go out of town on business, he realized that when he was young, he never felt that his mother paid enough attention to him except when he was sick. He recognized he had unconsciously adopted the habit of getting sick whenever he felt threatened by a lack of attention—and he had kept the pattern long after it had stopped working. That was the beginning.

Sometimes, we consciously adopt certain behaviors as a conceived plan of action—a way to handle a situation that feels out of control or to blunt physical or emotional pain. The problem is that this strategy stifles our happiness as effectively as it stifles the pain.

Another Story: In a seminar, Ann said she was raised in poverty and determined to succeed. She was a hard worker, and by the time she was twenty-five, she had put together the money and backers to buy a small boutique in Chicago. The belief she had adopted to pull herself up by her bootstraps was that she always had to work hard, solve problems, make improvements, and go at a project full steam ahead, or everything would crash and burn. Relaxing wasn't something she could even consider. It simply wasn't possible.

This is how she approached the new boutique. She worked around the clock, and sure enough, it was a huge success. Ann got what she wanted.

The problem arose when Ann discovered it wasn't easy to let go of this "full steam ahead" attitude. She feared that if she ever let up, all her success would vanish overnight, and she would feel terrible about herself. She had become a perfectionist. She couldn't rest until everything at home and work was in perfect order. She constantly pushed herself to do more, to find something that hadn't been done.

Ann realized she was not having fun with her life and had few friends left. Her women friends stopped calling her because she never came along with them. She was always too busy. Men found her exhausting and difficult to please. She began to see that she was out of balance with herself.

The very characteristic that had brought her success had become a part of her negative stress pattern. She had adopted the need to work and achieve to control her life, but now that same need was controlling *her*.

This story illustrates three points:
1. We need to reach a certain level of awareness to recognize areas of our lives that are out of balance. This in itself shows self-awareness growth.
2. We want to be gentle and forgiving with ourselves as we start to identify the patterns of negativity within us. We adopted these attitudes and behaviors for good reasons; in many cases, we needed them to survive. The problem is that we forgot to update ourselves and let go of these habits when they were no longer helpful. It's to our credit that we are doing that now.
3. The simple awareness of recognizing the area of negativity and targeting it for healing begins the process. Once we know what we want to focus on, some of the subtle work begins without us having to do much on the conscious level. Of course, there are many things we can and want to do beyond that initial recognition. Still, we can credit ourselves for having the courage to face very uncomfortable things.

Reflections

Can you identify stories and daydreams that may be based on fears, anger, victimhood, and sadness that are limiting you now?

Become aware of stories and traits you might wish to replace with self-confidence and optimism over the next period of time.

Reread the definitions of negativity to look for clues.

Chapter 10

Springboard?
Down to Up

CRISIS CAN LEAD to opportunity. We can view our forms of negativity as disguises. This is one of the Up Sides of Being Down. It teaches us to know ourselves better, transform negative into positive, and tap into mental powers we might never have used. It teaches us the art of making mistakes and correcting them. It shows us how to use symptoms as springboards for growth and benefit from what initially appear to be problems.

We've all heard the old expression, "It's not what you see that can hurt you; it's what you *can't* see." Those who haven't taken the time and energy to look at their personalities' negative, self-defeating aspects often find that those unconscious beliefs undermine them. We all have those parts of ourselves. Only when we look straight at them, with honesty and love, can we begin moving forward on our path of fulfillment—for ourselves and our possible contributions to the world. We can start to heal when we dare to look at our darker side. Those negative feelings don't sneak up on us as often, and we can recognize and refocus them when they do. It's trite but true to say that only when we have examined our dark side can we know our light.

As long as we deny the negativity within us,
it has power over our lives.

When we put all our energy into resisting the negativity or pretending it's not there, it controls us. That is where most of us have been. We cannot deal with what we refuse to see, so it festers beneath the surface, pulling our strings until we bring it into the light and look at it directly. This is when a good therapist or personal development support group can be meaningful to our growth. Though personal development is a subjective self-examination process, we often need others to mirror what they see in us. Within a safe therapeutic space, we can hear what we say and learn what we are feeling and thinking. We cannot see everything about ourselves by ourselves; it is too much a part of us.

Story: Beth was another overachiever who could never acknowledge her feelings of unworthiness. She had these feelings so well hidden behind the mask of her professional accomplishments that even *she* wasn't aware of them. Beth was an extraordinarily successful attorney—she had been appointed a judge before she turned thirty-five—but her personal life suffered. She maintained emotional distance from friends and had trouble connecting with men because, beneath all the success, she felt unlovable and unworthy.

She became so distressed with her failure on the personal side that she signed on for some therapy, where she got in touch with those subtle feelings of personal unworthiness. Once she could see the problem, she was off and running to fix it. She devoted her considerable energy to developing a self-directed Mind Fitness program emphasizing feeling lovable and deserving. She also sought counseling expertise to delve deeper into her past and discover how it affected her today.

Beth's initial experience of negativity turned out to be a gift. She uncovered a part of herself that was sabotaging her that might have stayed hidden if she hadn't felt the pain and done something about it. In the process, she also learned some strategies for continued personal development and tools she could use to deal with self-defeating attitudes and feelings in the future. Negativity can show us how we fall short of our higher aspirations—and where we need to work.

Using negativity as a teacher lets us turn these
self-sabotaging experiences into growth.

Reflections

Now is a good time to decide to focus on healing.

Sit quietly and focus on a time of confidence and gratitude.

Bask in this quiet self-acceptance.

Chapter 11

Where Are You?
Symptoms of Dis-Ease

THE UNDERLYING FEELING of all the symptoms of dis-ease is some form of recognized or unrecognized pain within ourselves. It is a pain we are trying to live with in some way. We may work to manage our emotional and psychological pain by resisting, dulling, hiding, chasing it away, projecting, or denying it. These forms of pain can become our way of getting through life the best way we know how. Many such pain-dodging responses, as said before, are early coping mechanisms in response to childhood events.

These means of surviving become limiting habits that underlie our negative thinking. They also can be elusive. They can hide behind symptoms of other conditions or seem to disappear entirely into the fabric of our lives. Sometimes, they are so pervasive that they can hardly be seen—we "can't see the forest for the trees." Everything we perceive is tinted. There are no rashes, bumps, or swellings in attitudinal disorders, but we indeed feel discomfort.

This list of symptoms may help pinpoint where you stand. It is intended only as a guideline. Having a few symptoms does not mean negativity has completely taken over your life. We aim to identify and recognize, then accept and forgive limiting patterns. From there, we can heal unwanted reactions by teaching ourselves new thinking patterns.

You may recognize characteristics on this list that have also been used to describe other newly named behavior syndromes. These "dysfunctions" are related to each other, with many of the identifying behaviors overlapping. Thus, speaking about generalized negativity is practical—this allows people to relearn and heal any beliefs, thoughts, or attitudes limiting their lives. They don't have to place the blame on themselves or anyone else or decide whether they were abused, addicted, children of alcoholics, co-dependent, a woman who loves too much, or whatever the form may be. They can begin to identify their limiting attitudes and thinking patterns, replacing those old, worn-out perceptions and beliefs with more empowering and expanding thinking.

Any cluster of attitudes or behaviors that diminish our aliveness and enjoyment of life is part of this syndrome. Those that follow are the ones people mention most often.

"That's Impossible"—The Habit of Defeatism

Those who are ruled by this habit approach most things as impossible. They place the burden on proving that it *might* be possible on someone else. The first reaction to new opportunities or situations is usually, "I couldn't do that." This self-defeating attitude of "I can't" or "I shouldn't" makes everything feel "too hard."

Judy always saw herself as inadequate and incapable of doing "anything important." She held conversations with herself that confirmed her worthlessness and incompetence. Right out loud, she said things like, "There, I've done it wrong again. I'm always so stupid . . . Look how I did that . . . I knew I wouldn't do it right."

This defeatist chatter became a self-fulfilling prophecy. Doing a good job is challenging when we sabotage everything we attempt. Even typical mistakes threw Judy into a tailspin and confirmed her already low opinion of herself.

Judy's recovery from the habit of defeatism began with recognizing and accepting her attitude. Once she understood that she had a habitual way of perceiving herself in the world and that this perception almost always worked to her detriment, she could begin to do something about it.

Judy shifted her focus to identifying and articulating what she did well, creating positive mental images and affirmations around her successes. She learned to acknowledge even the most minor accomplishment and to replace her sweeping, generalized perceptions of stupidity with more narrowly defined areas in which she experienced difficulty. Her inner mind work focused on recalling all the situations each day in which she had done an activity "right." This meant recognizing such taken-for-granted tasks as doing a good job at work, making dinner for guests, enjoying herself while she was out walking for exercise, stopping by to see her friend who was not feeling well, and so on. She developed a more honest picture of her abilities and talents from this. She began learning to assert her worth, which touched virtually every area of her life.

Sometimes, this habit of defeatist self-chatter can make even perfect situations feel bad. Betty constantly downed and disowned herself for being "scattered." She always came up with new ideas for social actions and improvements she could make in her community. One month, she would work on better ambulance service; the next month, she'd focus on a zoning crisis, a child-care facility, or a problem in the school system. She drowned herself because she didn't stay long with any one cause and was constantly moving around, never accomplishing anything that changed the world.

Betty wanted to perceive herself in a way that would be more integrated and fulfilling. The key for her was finding the common thread running through all of her work.

As she pictured herself in her mind's eye, she began to see a circle with herself in the middle. All around her were the various causes she was involved in. She began to see that she was an essential catalyst for all these causes and that her job was to keep moving and catalyzing change. The self-definition that bridged her activities and integrated her work was a "catalyst for social good."

Instead of thinking about how the ambulance, school, or childcare people would perceive her (as one who was only partly involved), she began concentrating on how she perceived *herself*. Putting herself at the center of the circle and permitting herself to adopt the self-definition of "catalyst for social good" integrated the various activities in her life and let her take on more of them without guilt or self-chatter.

The part of the story I love is that Betty went on to become mayor of her suburban town and is now *really* making changes to a wide range of the community's departments!

"I Am Having a Conniption Fit" —Anger or Depression

These are well-known symptoms to many people. Anger and depression both stem from fear. Anger results when the emotions are turned outward toward others; depression often results when they are turned inward against ourselves. If we are in the habit of blaming others, we are more likely to be angry. If we are in the habit of feeling guilty or unworthy, we are more likely to be depressed.

I am not talking about clinical depression here, which is best treated with medication and therapy, and I am not suggesting that we should never feel angry or depressed. These are normal human emotions that we all experience from time to time that can spur growth. What I am talking about is a level of low-level depression and anger that stays with us for long periods of time. This is the kind of anger or depression that is inclined to color our perceptions and attitudes in unhappy ways.

Some of the situations that prompt anger or depression are:
- Feeling powerless, out of control, or unable to cope.
- Feeling unable to get our way.
- Hearing people say things we don't like or want to hear.
- Thinking that others have violated our rights or that someone has taken advantage of us.
- Feeling unappreciated or unacknowledged.
- Having an experience that reminds us of early childhood events in which we felt particularly powerless, angry, or fearful.

It's essential to identify and deal with our anger or depression for three reasons:
1. Sometimes, anger or depression that is unrecognized or suppressed takes the form of generalized hostility. Everything

has a negative twist. Whether we lash out or maintain a stony silence, the message is "Stay away from me." This inhibits love and growth and puts a wall around us that keeps out much of life.

2. When anger is denied or allowed to fester unattended, it can burst forth unexpectedly and violently, harming ourselves or others.

3. Research shows that people who are chronically angry or depressed tend to develop physical ailments and diseases. Cancer is the disease mentioned most often. Cancer involves a rampant overproduction of destructive cells that attack the body, much as an angry individual randomly attacks people he knows. Anger is indeed physically toxic.

We think of depression as sadness, but it is more often simply a *depressing*, or shutting down, of all our systems—physical, mental, emotional, and spiritual—almost as if we were in hibernation or walking through molasses. We can feel heavy and overwhelmed by life to the point that we want to curl up into a ball and hide.

Physical and mental pain can be deeply connected. Our bodies become storehouses for the negativity generated by our thoughts and attitudes. Sooner or later, this affects our physical health, which affects our psychological health. It becomes a vicious cycle. Chronic *fears* about our health can produce the same result.

We all know angry, negative people who wear the marks of these attitudes on their faces in the form of deep frown lines and downturned mouths. We have seen pessimistic people who feel victimized and burdened, walking around with stooped backs, looking as if they were physically weighed down and overloaded. On the other hand, we all know joyful and optimistic people whose bodies reflect openness, flexibility, and adaptability. They move easily and gracefully, and their smiles reflect inner peace and strength. There is a warmth about them.

Anger and depression are two of the most challenging aspects of personal negativity because they feel so powerful and out of control. The Mind Fitness philosophy emphasizes learning to listen to our intuitive selves clearly and honestly and trusting in the process. By encouraging self-determination in our focus, we learn to let go of the helpless feelings that often prompt anger.

"Melancholy, Cry Baby"—Sadness

This, too, is a normal human emotion that only becomes problematic when it becomes extreme, pervasive, or chronic.

If a loved one has just died, we expect to feel sad—for quite a while. In the wake of a personal trauma like losing a job or a forced move to a different part of the country, we have a right to grieve. Many experts now realize that we need to grieve whenever there is a significant change in our lives. We grieve for the old, even when the new thing is something positive—the birth of a baby, promotion to a new job, or marriage to a wonderful new spouse.

We need to allow ourselves these kinds of sadness and mourning. Still, we don't want to let sadness or melancholy become the base from which we operate—or an excuse never to try anything new or to challenge ourselves. In other words, when sorrow and self-pity keep us from taking responsibility for our lives and happiness, we may have crossed the line into just plain feeling sorry for ourselves.

When Richard lost his middle-management job at a computer company, it was a tremendous shock to him and his family. His wife Sally had a good position, but their two children were in private schools, and the family could barely scrape by on her salary. Richard took a few weeks off before looking for a new job to get his feet on the ground emotionally and take what he considered a well-earned vacation.

He had been an overachiever all his life, and losing this job was a sharp blow to his ego. Richard's emotional tailspin took the form not of anger, regret, or guilt but of a slow-burning, somewhat bitter sadness. At first, he lay around the house, reading, then doing practically nothing. Soon, he hardly had the energy to get out of bed in the morning unless Sally prodded him before she left for work. Nothing seemed to matter to him. The sadness had become a wall that protected him from everything else.

Finally, Sally's patience and the family finances reached a crisis point, and Richard sought help. He realized that the main thing his sadness kept him from feeling was *failure*. That was the one thing he had never wanted to experience, and here it was, right in his face. In fact, he hadn't failed—his firing had stemmed from cutbacks, not poor performance—but "failure" was the name Richard attached to losing one's job.

Richard also realized he could never move forward and get a new job if he didn't take responsibility his disappointment and sadness. **Mind Fitness techniques enabled Richard to:**

- **RELAX** with awareness and get to a place where he was more truthful with himself.
- **VISUALIZE** what he wanted based on his values and ways to get there.
- **AFFIRM**, in words, what was positive and working in his life right now and what skills he had to offer.

Through this process, he began to accept his strengths and weaknesses as part of being human and began to regain his balance in life. Within a month, he found a job he liked and felt a new sense of confidence and vitality.

"The Tough One"—Criticism, Cynicism, and Righteousness

The clever person often manifests insecurities by striving to appear better than anyone else. The hallmarks of this symptom are witty, sarcastic, or critical remarks that put down or make fun of everything and everyone.

People who demonstrate this form of negativity find it hard to resist taking potshots at others—and sometimes at themselves. They adopt "class clown" behavior rather than admit their underlying lack of self-esteem. By making cynical jokes and putting things down, they develop an identity that gets them the attention they crave . . . but it's not the kind of attention they seek. Often, they have an unconscious belief that if others get ahead, they will be left behind—that if others win, they will lose. They want to seem superior so they won't lose their edge, which often takes the form of being highly critical.

I was once called into a corporate setting to work with a man whom management valued highly. He did excellent work but was so sarcastic that his coworkers did not want him on their team. This man was brilliant at seeing people's weakest points and letting them have it with some clever, demeaning remark. His intelligence was high, but his generosity of spirit was lacking, and he was hurtful to others. He told me he "needed to be tough, or others would get to him." It's tough for people with that mindset to be generous or forgiving. He said he didn't want to be considered "soft" or "stupid."

People who rely on this pattern of criticism, cynicism, and righteousness find it difficult to break for two reasons:

- They are often successful, bright, and outgoing. Their identity is tied up in their verbal brightness. They usually think their intelligence is responsible for whatever social success they have achieved, and they are afraid that they will lose their edge if they stop publicly snipping and demeaning others with witty or cutting remarks.

- They realize that other people enjoy their Don Rickles-type performance and don't want the practitioners to give up their "routines" because they are entertaining. One seminar participant came back later and told me, "My friends all say, 'I liked you better when you were cutting, sarcastic, and cynical!'"

Tough cookie: Another aspect of this pattern is the emotionally closed "tough cookie" veneer. Alice told us that she was the oldest child in her family, and when she was growing up, she was responsible for babysitting the three younger children. She felt as if she was always taking care of everybody's needs. Around age sixteen, she rebelled. Her formerly sweet and docile nature took on a bitter, sarcastic edge that bordered on being nasty. She began being purposely mean to the younger kids so her mother was afraid to leave them with her. It worked. Since she was no longer trusted, she didn't have to assume responsibility for anyone's care.

Her hostility got Alice out of being the family's "little mother," but as she turned thirty, she realized that other people were just as put off by the chip on her shoulder as her family had been. She had difficulty establishing friendships, was seldom involved in relationships, and was inclined to have trouble with coworkers. The behavior that had worked so well when she was a teen was no longer working to her advantage, and Alice didn't know how to "turn it off," or even that it would benefit her to.

As she became aware of what had happened, she was gradually able to let the "tough cookie" act go and began to rebuild her gentler, more caring nature.

"Seeing Through Gray-Colored Glasses"—Pessimism

This is the attitude that things probably *won't* turn out for the best—or even if they do, the result will still be a downer and somewhat painful. Pessimism can become a filter through which we see everything in life, an attitude of "guilty until proven innocent" rather than "innocent until proven guilty." Everything is a drag. We are quicker to see the Down Side than the Up Side.

Sometimes, we do this to protect ourselves from disappointment. Our expectations are more likely to be met if they are low. If we don't think the relationship will work out or that we will get the raise or the promotion, then we won't be as disappointed or hurt when those things don't happen.

Of course, we set up a series of self-fulfilling prophecies. Pessimism doesn't usually foster personal or professional success; so then we have even more reason to be pessimistic next time we fall short of our expectations.

Ralph found himself in this position with women. "The women I find attractive are never interested in me," he said. With this attitude, he approached every date defensively, expecting either to be uninterested in the woman or to be rejected. His lack of confidence and "beaten puppy" demeanor did nothing to enhance his effect on women. He was a living example of the old Groucho Marx line, "I wouldn't want to belong to any club that would have me as a member."

Ralph's habit of pessimism caught him in a downward spiral. When he began to recognize his fears of rejection, he began to visualize other ways of handling various situations. Using his imagination skills, he "rehearsed" what it would mean to be willing to approach each relationship as if it actually might work. He experienced greater peace of mind, and his social life took a turn for the better.

"The Regulator"—A High Need for Control

This high need for control can take many forms: perfectionism at work; immaculate standards, from personal hygiene to housekeeping; safe relationships; rigid viewpoints; fears of change; compulsive behaviors and phobias; any set of attitudes that limit the boundaries of our own or others' speech or actions.

Some people in our seminars describe this desperate need for control as feeling out of control, helpless, and "barely hanging on." We're afraid that if we ever stop holding everything up, it will all crash around our shoulders; if we don't nail everything down, it will blow away; left to its own devices, the world will go awry.

Renee noticed her unusually high need for control when an old college friend from out of town visited. Renee was forty-two and had lived alone since her divorce at age thirty-five. Everything in her condo had an established place, just as everything on her desk at work was set up just so.

Trouble began almost as soon as Renee's friend Evelyn arrived in Seattle for a long weekend. Not only did Evelyn put things back in the wrong place after doing the dishes; she also left splashes around the bathroom sink, and she was angry when Renee wouldn't let her borrow her car.

After Evelyn left, Renee started seeing herself through her old friend's eyes and realized she had become compulsive. She was the only person she knew, for instance, who never let other people borrow her car.

As she spent some time in quiet, proactive reflection, Renee realized that much of her need for control came from feeling *out of control*. She wanted to be in a relationship and didn't seem to be able to make that happen. She wanted a house but never had enough for a down payment.

Just recognizing the problem took much of the pressure off, and Renee could start working on the real issues. Self-doubt is usually a part of that out-of-control feeling. When we stop trusting that we can handle the situation and begin to doubt ourselves, we open the door to fearful thoughts that can ambush us when we least expect it. We become tentative and close ourselves off from positive opportunities because we fear they won't work out.

Just as self-doubts can bring about an attack of negativity, an infusion of self-confidence can transform it. In the second part of this book, we will discuss how to turn self-doubt into confidence by taking a few minutes daily for inner attention.

"Mis-matched"—Internal and External Realities Don't Match

We say we're "just fine," but we know we're not. We say nothing is wrong, but, in fact, nothing seems right. We look fine on the outside but feel tormented on the inside. We are not telling the truth. We don't want to bother people; we want things to look "just fine." We are playing a game of social illusion.

There are variations: We may feel OK at home, but our world falls apart when we go to work. Conversely, we may feel okay at work and be unhappy and overwhelmed at home. We may even behave quite differently in the two places.

We get our ideas of who we should be and what we should be doing from other people rather than from our values, letting who we are and what we want to be doing emerge from within. Because we get clues about how we should be from the external world, our minds tell us one thing, and our emotions experience another. We are mismatched and out of sorts.

"Shifty"—Restlessness and Difficulty Focusing

This feeling that there is no center to our activities can happen at work, home, or both. We feel scattered, rushed, overloaded, and hopeless about ever getting it all done. We keep changing directions and need help with finishing tasks. We often set our goals too high, so nothing seems attainable, and we almost don't feel like trying. It's high stress and anxiety.

"I was lucky just to make it through the day, let alone accomplish anything or have any fun," says Maggie, who manages a household and works part-time for an accountancy firm. "It was a struggle to stay centered because I wasn't putting myself in the middle of this fast-spinning wheel. I was overwhelmed and felt pulled in a million directions. I had no idea where *I* wanted to go."

Maggie still does many of the same things and has the same schedule. Still, she has learned how to prioritize her activities, allowing her to go through each day with more of a sense of control, balance, and, yes, even some feelings of completion rather than scattered frustration.

Satisfaction has less to do with our activities and the people or circumstances outside ourselves than how we feel about ourselves. I've spoken with corporate executives, doctors, therapists, and others who have accomplished much in the world's eyes and greatly impacted other people's lives. Yet they don't feel much satisfaction in their work. And I've spoken with other people whose contributions are less esteemed and who experience pride and satisfaction in doing repetitively mundane things. Of course, some highly successful people love their work, some chafe in their everyday jobs, and let's face it . . . some jobs and chores are just the pits. My point is that some of our working life satisfaction comes from within us, and some of it comes from outside of us. The Up Side is we can work on our inner satisfaction even when we cannot change the external demands. Is it easy? Rarely, but it's possible.

My satisfaction rule of thumb is that I am in good shape if I like doing something about four days out of five. We all have bad days, but when we experience chronic disappointment and dissatisfaction—when we are dissatisfied more than we are satisfied—something is wrong.

"It Ain't My Fault"—Feeling Victimized

We all know people who go through life as "professional victims." Nothing ever really works for them—love, money, job, family, you name it—and it's always someone else's fault. If no specific person or situation is to blame, they'll blame "fate, luck, the times, or society."

In its exaggerated form, this symptom means feeling like something is out to get us, and the best we can do is react and dodge the next bullet ("I was just lying there, and the train came by and hit me!")

It's a painful way to go through life and doesn't lead to much happiness or growth. However, there *are* ways to deal with this feeling and replace it with attitudes that embrace life and its challenges.

"I'm Not Okay, and Neither Are You"—Guilt

When we notice that guilt has become the coin of our realm—the thing we use to pay people and demand from them in return—it's time to stop and see what's going on.

When we feel guilty or want the people around us to feel guilty, it's a clue that we don't feel terrific about ourselves. Some form of blackness has gotten a foothold somewhere, and we need to focus our attention on it.

Rachel, the mother of three grown children, realized that most of her time was spent either feeling guilty about how she had raised them or trying to make them feel guilty that they hadn't fulfilled all her expectations.

She explained, "I realized that the only way for me not to feel guilty was to make *them* feel guilty. *Somebody* had to feel guilty; that's the way I was raised. Better them than me—except then, I didn't want to see them hurt, so I'd take back the guilt myself.

"Finally, I took the big step and decided to see what would happen if we just took the whole guilt thing out of the equation so *nobody* had to feel guilty. It was initially strange for us all, and change didn't happen overnight. We all felt uneasy because it was so different. But now we're getting used to it and like it better."

The Smart Dis-Ease

It often seems that people who are particularly "smart," who have had the most success in their intellectually oriented educational system, are the most prone to negativity. Often, there is a sniper effect; they subtly put down others—"put them in their place"—as if pushing others down will make them more successful. As I described in "The Tough One," they can't resist taking potshots disguised as humor, when, in fact, they are demeaning others' abilities or skills. When this is pointed out, they often reply, "I was only joking!" These are learned behaviors, and "smart" people are good at learning, but I think it goes deeper than that.

Our schools and society promote analytical left-brain thinking, and some intellectually astute people get so in the habit of thinking only with the rational part of their minds that they develop an extremely critical, analytical approach to everything. They have a mindset that challenges any new person or idea: "Prove to me that you're worthwhile." They immediately examine any unique idea for all the reasons it won't work and bombard the person who suggested it with all the rational reasons why it will fail. They toss a wet blanket over the idea before anyone can consider that it might work or be valuable. With its possibilities cut down by cynicism, the idea never has a chance to germinate.

We all know people who operate like this. Nothing is ever good enough. Nothing ever meets with their wholehearted approval. They can always see something that will go wrong; that is where they focus. At best, such people acknowledge that something just might be acceptable, but they make sure we know there is much to criticize.

The emphasis on rational inquiry fosters this attitude of negation. If you ask these people to watch a movie, they either don't want to see it because it hasn't gotten good reviews, or they go with you and rip it to shreds. The dinner was good, but too bad the vegetables weren't hot. They want to lose weight but "can't" because people are constantly forcing them to go out and eat fattening things. They make a full-time occupation by poking holes in things and cutting people down to size. "Yes, that woman is nice, but too bad she never accomplished much in her life." "Yes, that man has a good business but is not very nice."

It's as if they're afraid that if they ever let anything get by without pointing out its faults, they wouldn't appear smart enough, discriminating enough, or astute enough. This habit often starts because people don't feel very good about themselves, and school is where they've achieved success and won approval. They feel most comfortable in this intellectual, highly critical arena. It's their turf. It's where they win, where they look good, and where they feel worthwhile and valuable.

Often, when these people start practicing a form of inner focusing, they discover creative parts of themselves that are worthwhile, valuable, and lovable. They find they can afford to relax a little and accept things and people who are less than perfect. No longer must they push others down to feel up. They begin using and appreciating life with their right brains as well as with their left brains and find out that adding the right brain makes them not only more imaginative and more creative but also more accepting. They are unafraid to say, "I don't know; let's find out." For the first time, they develop internal unity and balance. They discover that they don't have to give up their intellectual life at all; they can *enhance* it with a more intuitive, imaginative, and creative side of themselves, letting them enjoy life more and be more expressive.

Story: Ethel had worked in public relations in New York for twenty years, moving to San Diego when her husband was transferred. For the first year, being in California made her crazy. She thought everyone she met was a "fuzz-brain." No one read the papers or books. They didn't know what was happening in the world—and worse, they didn't seem to care. They talked about their feelings, watched sunsets, and ate kiwi fruit. They seemed to have no logical functioning and were completely undiscriminating in their artistic tastes. Ethel was sure no one in the state had an IQ of more than 80. It's not too hard to see her negative taproot.

But what made Ethel nuts was how people talked about their "processes." They loved to remember things that happened when they were children, go over all the feelings they had, all the anger and hurt, and talk about how that might have affected the way they were today. They couldn't seem to get enough of it. Every time Ethel heard one of these conversations, she blew her stack. Her inner talk went, "This is so juvenile, so stupid, so weak and wishy-washy."

In fact, Ethel herself had had a painful childhood. Her parents had been involved in an unpleasant divorce, and she had felt torn between them, never feeling like she had a home with either of them. The thought of mentally returning and allowing herself to experience those feelings was terrifying. The idea that they might have something to do with the rather harsh person she had become made her question her identity and feel out of control.

No wonder it made her so uncomfortable when people talked about these feeling-oriented, "airy-fairy" things. Ethel liked objective things that could be measured, understood, and eliminated if they didn't measure up or make sense. The things these people were talking about were subjective and didn't make sense. They seemed to turn her world upside down.

Nevertheless, Ethel's education and intelligence worked in her favor. She realized that if she had such an intense and irrational response to something, she should probably examine it. She took the time to look at why these types of conversations upset her, realized that they were triggering some of her old emotions, and began taking steps to deal with her abandonment and anger issues. She started to find words for her feelings.

As she continued to include a daily time of Mind Fitness, Ethel began to see other ways of viewing herself. She realized that she didn't need to rely entirely on her left brain; she could allow some of the softer, more intuitive, emotional parts of herself to surface. She began to feel less threatened and, therefore, to be less critical. She began to understand that past events didn't have to dictate who she was; she was now an adult and could choose her attitudes and life responses.

People who fall prey to negativity because they are intelligent and well-educated in analytical skills are usually also smart enough to eventually see what it is doing to them and to understand that they don't have to be negative and unhappy just because they have been blessed with high intelligence.

Reflections

I bet you already know what this reflection will be...so go ahead, take some time to identify which of the symptoms you might be carrying in your daily life. Most of us have more than one and surely there are some that you may identify that I have not named.

It is also helpful to go the extra step and rank the symptoms if there are more than a couple. That will help you to decide what to focus your inner mind sessions on first. Remember this is personal inner work and need not be shared with others; Mind Fitness is your own approach to life, not anyone else's which is why I am not sharing mine with you!

1.

2.

3.

4.

Chapter 12

The Payoffs

WHY DO WE behave in self-sabotaging ways? What could we get from letting ourselves drift into these negative states? Could there be payoffs for our avoidance behavior?

It's not easy to look at what these payoffs might be; in fact, it can be downright embarrassing, even to ourselves. But the advantage to discovering how we avoid our pain is that we can make choices. We can see if the payoffs are still worth it or if we're operating automatically based on past needs that aren't relevant any longer. Examining whether we can accept and then move past our initial pain opens up new avenues of increased balance and fullness. Are we now receiving as much from the payoffs as we might if we gave up the particular symptoms that we manifest and lived more fully and joyfully?

Each one of us has different payoffs for different symptoms.
Watch as you go through your days and weeks to see where these avoidance strategies may be in play for you. We have all adapted our forms of personal negativity to fit our perceived "needs" and to ensure our emotional survival. It may look different in each of us, but three common threads run through most people's negativity payoffs:

1. **Avoiding responsibility.** There is no need to do anything or risk anything if someone or something else is always to blame. By blaming everything outside of ourselves, in a constant stream of whines, complaints, and angry jabs, we put off from

ourselves any responsibility for change or positive actions and place it firmly on the shoulders of the outside world. Who are we? Just poor little us. We have no control. With this thinking, we can justify lazy inertia, rather than risk-taking actions, and complaining, creating anger rather than action or peace.

2. **Avoiding commitment.** As long as we see the world filled with impossibilities, we don't have to work hard, commit to anything, or demonstrate our abilities. Our attitude is, "Why run the race if you aren't going to win it?" "It's not going to work anyway, so why try?" We never have to fail if we avoid committing to challenges. To commit ourselves to a goal means taking a position that requires sustained energy and proactive strategies for success. Saying "Why bother?" gets us out of a lot of work, keeps us from stretching our limits, and feeds into a lazy and self-centered mindset. It robs us of the satisfactions of action towards success.

3. **Avoiding intimacy.** Staying prickly, irritated, and sullen allows us to hide from others and remain sealed in our little world. We don't have to face the challenges of sharing ourselves and being vulnerable if we are always "looking down our noses on others," finding no one else worthy of our respect. Being superior is a sure way of remaining separate. Being intimate with someone means we are willing to be equal with others in a respectful and mutual manner. If we push others away, we can stay uninvolved; we don't have to act on behalf of anyone but ourselves. Negativity prevents us from connecting with others and keeps us locked in our self-justifying and blaming mindset.

Hiding and numbing pain takes a lot of different forms. We all have ways of avoiding it by expressing negativity with a combination of payoffs, but it's a good bet that most of the symptoms manifest in one or more variations of these three. Recognizing this is critical to growth and healing. Still, we must not make this recognition one more cause for self-recrimination—we must keep in mind that these developed patterns of personal negativity are ways of protecting ourselves and coping with emotional pain or stress.

Choosing Your Focus

In these chapters, we've discussed how these habit patterns may have started and some specific symptoms. It's unlikely that anyone manifests *all* these symptoms; some may have symptoms that are not mentioned here. This list is only a guideline to help you begin to watch your own behaviors that may be in the limiting sabotaging category. These symptoms may help identify the specific areas on which to focus as we get ready to heal patterns of defeated thinking. We must recognize the aspects of our lives that we want to start healing and keep those areas in mind as we learn more about this condition and how to reverse it.

Reflections

Most of us can admit to avoiding all three of the avoidance payoffs at different times and with different people and situations.

Take a few deep breaths to center and relax yourself. This is always the starting place. Allow your body and mind to just rest for a while.

As you go through your days, keep in mind the three avoidances: responsibility, commitment, and intimacy and see how they may or may not play a part in your life.

Chapter 13

Are You Ready?
The Three Stages of Healing

Healing and learning to see with the power of optimism begin the moment we recognize our negative patterns and choose to break that cycle. This is the hardest part—looking directly at our attitudes and behaviors and realizing how they limit us. The Up Side is that once we know what we are doing, we can opt to learn new ways of behaving . . . at least most of the time.

Three Stages
We can heal personal negativity by taking these three steps:
1. **Recognize** what is wrong.
2. **Accept and forgive** ourselves for not being perfect.
3. **Heal** the condition.

Let's look at each of these steps.

1. Identify and Recognize. To some people, this is an unnecessary step. We already recognize what's wrong: *we feel awful.* Our lives are not working.

However, have we identified precisely what the problem is? Identification is giving things a label. Labeling puts a name to something we now recognize as a limiting part of us holding us back. Negativity shows up differently in each of us. We must do our personal watching and soul-searching to pinpoint precisely how it manifests in our lives. The clearer we get, the easier it will be to heal the condition. What *exactly* is wrong? Make clear to yourself as precisely as possible what you wish to change to heal.

Another reason it's essential to be specific about what feels out of balance is that many forms of limited, painful, and fearful thinking tend to be "hidden." They are subtle and insidious and usually exist for years before we recognize and own them. And because there has been no name until now, it has been challenging to get a handle on anything meaningful. Acknowledging negatives has not been a part of our culture—something that people share—so most of us have hidden many subtle and not-so-subtle negative feelings for fear of being criticized or feeling all alone. Now, we are discovering that this affects people in all walks of life and at every level of success.

The following questions are helpful in identifying just how the taproot of this condition shows up in our lives:

- Am I more often unhappy than happy?
- Do I feel angry or upset even when, in reality, my physical environment is acceptable?
- Do I overreact to people who disagree with me?
- Do I snap at people unnecessarily on some days and seem much more patient on others?
- Do I wake up feeling stressed out before I even open my eyes?
- Do I wonder if I can get through each day?
- Do I feel rushed most of the time?
- Am I more able to keep myself together with strangers than with my family? Am I generally inconsistent in my moods and interactions with people?
- Do I sleep more than I need to, sit staring into space, feeling down and sluggish, or work more than I need to and in a pressured way?
- Do I feel picked on and abused by life?
- Do I feel sad, complaining, or judgmental more often than the conditions in my life warrant?
- Do I find focusing my attention and activities challenging and often feel scattered and incomplete?

- Do I feel tense, anxiously "fighting the clock" most of the time?
- Are most of my first impressions and reactions to people, situations, or new ideas negative?
- Do I feel nothing is ever good enough?
- Is my vocabulary more hostile than gentle? What kinds of words do I use most frequently? Are they supportive, expansive words, or are they more shut down, pessimistic, angry, or defeatist?
- Do I replay negative, upsetting scenes in my mind, feeling increasingly angry or powerless?

You may answer "No" to all of these questions and still feel that you suffer from destructive Down moods and attitudes. If you don't feel these questions have identified how unsatisfying moods and attitudes manifest in your life, take a few minutes to jot down some of your own ideas.

2. Accept and Forgive. The second step is to stop self-justification, admit we're imperfect, and forgive ourselves. We recognize and accept that we have some negative, self-defeating attitudes and behaviors that are causing us to live less fulfilling lives than we otherwise would—and we can change these negative, self-defeating attitudes and behaviors.

It's easy to blame others by saying, "I'm the way I am because of how my parents raised me. If they'd done things differently, I'd have a happier, more productive life," or "If I hadn't been abused, I would be softer and gentler," or "If had hadn't been abandoned, I could trust more."

It's easy to say, "I can't help it that I've had a tragic life—those things just happened, and I was the victim of Fate."

It's easy to say, "If my neighborhood had been better and my parents had had a good relationship, then I'd be able to have one too," or "If my parents had taught me about money, I wouldn't have all these problems."

Life might indeed be easier given different "what-ifs," and causes beyond our control may seem to take us off the hook, but denial and excuses only prolong negative thinking, making it more difficult to do anything about the situation now. If we keep placing blame outside ourselves, we know we are still in denial. We can choose to play an active role in *un*-creating our excuses and replacing them with new, more positive attitudes and

79

behaviors. We do this as we accept that our foundational attitudes are learned and created by us, knowingly or unknowingly; therefore, we can learn new ones.

We can't always control what happens in our lives, but we have choices about how we respond. Life does throw some "wild cards" at us—and we all cope as best we can. As we know from our own experiences with personal loss and tragedy, disagreement, separation, and death are painful parts of life. The challenge is not letting them defeat us. Instead we must accept, incorporate, and grow from them, drawing renewed meaning and more profound compassion into our lives.

As we begin taking responsibility for our part in our negativity, it's helpful to ask these questions:

- Am I filling my life with more difficulties or blame than necessary?
- Might some of my problems be self-inflicted?
- Could I have reacted more positively to some of the significant changes that have taken place in my life? Is it possible that I've been harboring resentment for a long time?
- Now that I think about it, did I spend a lot of time imagining negative scenes as a youngster?
- Do I dwell on thoughts and feelings that aren't conducive to happiness or growth?
- Do I find it hard to feel happy?

Once we have identified the problem and accepted that we are part of it, we can begin the healing process.

3. Heal. We choose to heal; we set our minds to learning new, more positive attitudes and behaviors. We do this by taking responsibility for our moods and attitudes and then consciously and actively employing the same techniques we have used unconsciously to set these patterns in motion. We put our minds into training. This philosophy and way of living is based on self-esteem and belief in ourselves and our experiences. It is a new way of thinking about ourselves and what is possible for us based on optimism and self-determination.

It means:

- Actively listening to our intuition—the quiet inner self that is wiser than the outer, surface self could ever be.
- Shifting our thinking from snap judgments and automatic reactions to fuller, richer ways of looking at and reacting to things.
- Consciously clarifying and focusing on who we want to be and how we want to live our lives.
- Seeing life from a new perspective, based on love and growth rather than on past helplessness, anger, and fear.

Healing, in this book, means removing the fear-based, negative "That won't work . . . they are to blame . . . I can do it better" filter that has colored our perceptions of things in life and seeing with optimism, expansion, and possibility. It means releasing the Down Side by focusing on the Up Side by experiencing the best potential in ourselves and others. This is not an overnight process, but we can do it when we choose to begin.

Reflections

This chapter has plenty of questions for you to reflect upon. Take the time to answer them thoroughly and thoughtfully. Mind Fitness is inner personal work so don't be afraid to be honest with yourself.

Chapter 14

Scared?
The Moment of Decision

THERE COMES A moment when we recognize the stranglehold that negative attitudes and thinking have on our lives. At that point, we have to decide what, if anything, we are going to do about it.

The various forms of personal negativity are habits of fear-based thought. The adrenaline rush we may get from them can make them as addictive as cigarettes, alcohol, drugs, or food. We need as much courage to overcome habits of negative perception as we do to take on better-known physical addictions.

Most people need time to build up to this moment of decision—the turning point at which we commit to begin to heal ourselves of some of our forms of negativity. But at some point, everything mysteriously comes together, and we are ready. It's as if the water finally starts to boil after being heated. All our energies seem to come together. We are very clear on what we want, and we muster the courage, the commitment, the will, and the strength to make that decision last through all the temptations that come up.

Our habits of negative thinking have been built up over many years, and they aren't going to disappear overnight. What we are talking about here is not a promise that self-defeating thoughts will never surface again, but a commitment to ourselves to work with them when they do—a decision to make an effort to learn something from each experience while focusing on teaching ourselves more empowered thinking.

This is an attitude-to-action approach.

Most of us have committed to something similar to this. It may have concerned an addiction, relationship, or behavior pattern. When it is time to move on something, there is a moment of drawing in the breath, straightening the spine, and letting a solid determination rise to the surface: a decision to give up some form of self-sabotage, no matter how uncomfortable that may make us in the short term; a determination to relinquish parts of our less-evolved natures for a fuller knowledge and appreciation of our higher possibilities. It is a moment of deep faith in ourselves, a moment of radical trust, a moment of surrender and acceptance that sometimes gives us the feeling of being out of control. The irony is that in committing ourselves, we gain more control over our lives than we have ever experienced.

One thing that makes us resist commitment is that human beings don't like change—even good change. It's uncomfortable not to be who we always were, even if our expansion lets us experience and enjoy life more fully. To break out of one way of doing things and cross over into another is a risky, scary thing to do. It takes great personal courage.

When the change has to do with growth, it's even scarier.

When we admit that we want to get better, there's an implication that things aren't so good now. If friends say, "You look more relaxed than I've ever seen you before," we must admit that we looked tense and uptight in the past. If they say, "Hey, you look wonderful!" we suspect that maybe we didn't look so good before.

We can also get caught up in the syndrome of "As long as I stay just mediocre, I won't be noticed." A woman from Ohio once told me she was afraid to dress nicely because she would look "too sexy and good, and then people would notice me. I never know what to say when people fuss over me." She was embarrassed by the attention she'd gotten when she dressed well and felt she didn't know how to handle public admiration, so she hid behind dowdy, nondescript clothes.

There are ways to hide that don't involve clothing. We hide from things we fear. We may hide from commitment, standing out, intimacy, and admitting we made a mistake. That's why it takes such great courage to commit to ourselves—to risk breaking out of the habit of defeat, blame, and anger to create a fuller way of living for ourselves. Some parts of ourselves would rather be comfortable with what we know. There is a fear of changing, even if it means feeling fulfilled and successful. It takes breaking out of our old patterns, perhaps even a certain laziness, to sustain a committed energy for our well-being and health. We want to acknowledge and be gentle with all parts of ourselves, knowing we've decided not to hold ourselves back.

The author and lecturer Hugh Prather reminded us how strong that pull to the negative is when he said in one of his talks:

"The ego loves to be a martyr."

Reflections

Take a few breaths and allow yourself to feel resistance—we all have it.

Can you make the decision to give yourself a time of mindful quieting and self-reflection?

When you are ready, say "Yes!" to yourself.

PART 2

Let's Go!
Mind Fitness for Healing

We are now expanding our thinking as individuals and as a society to recognize that care and "exercise" for the mind is as essential for human health and well-being as care and exercise for the body.

Chapter 15

A Quiet Place

THE PRACTICE OF relaxation and inner listening is more accessible if we have an imaginary special place within us to which we go. I call this the "personal template of relaxation." It is just a place we imagine within ourselves, with all the sensations we feel when we are actually in that place. It might be a beach, mountain top, sunlit meadow, comfortable living room, forest, lake, river, or just a hammock in the garden.

Take a few minutes to imagine a place that you know and love. Imagine an environment where you feel at peace, comfortable, and serene. Feel the calmness of relaxation wash over you. This is where you will mentally begin your time-out session each day—your inner retreat ritual. It may take a few days to get used to this being your quiet mental place. (You can choose a new relaxation place at any time.) Each time you revisit a mental image of your special place, you will relax more quickly and easily.

Setting up a special physical place in your home for mental reflection is helpful.

Just taking the time to establish this as your place is meaningful. You tell yourself you have decided to heal and grow by spending time in proactive reflection and quiet.

Some people can set aside an entire room as their place for inner mind work. We used a small room for this purpose when we lived in Hawaii. It was the "quiet room." We went there to do our inner work whenever we felt the need to be calm and at peace spiritually. In that room, we felt protected until we could find a fuller light within ourselves. Sometimes, when we were hosting a party, I would discover a guest hidden away in the quiet room. It was a place to reach decisions simply by relaxing and reflecting. By its presence, the little room reminded us to take time for inner work, giving us a haven during the process.

Most people use part of a room, perhaps a corner or shelf, for their special place. Now that we live in a smaller house, I use a small chest to place personal, meaningful things. Each of us can create a special place that is our private temple. In our special place, we can have symbols that inspire us: pictures, statues, flowers, shells, prayers, written affirmations, and personally meaningful tokens. Each time we walk by our quiet place, we are reminded of our dedication to expanding our lives and fulfilling our highest potential. We're also reminded of the larger universe and our relation to the whole.

When I travel, I take a special place with me. I carry a small scarf as a table covering, a few pictures of my family, and some items from my home. No matter where I am, as soon as I set up my special place, I have a wonderful sense of being grounded and at home.

A friend told me that he took a few special objects and pictures to Moscow and set them up on the nightstand in his hotel room. The next day, he came back in the middle of the afternoon to find three of the floor women gathered in his room, looking at his special place and admiring the objects he had there. They were very embarrassed and scurried out quickly, but later, one returned and apologized. She spoke a bit of English and said, "This is very special to you, no?" He replied with a simple "Yes." From that day on, although it was the middle of February and flowers were expensive and hard to find in Moscow, a fresh flower was always placed on his table.

There is a specific power in ritual.

Before going to sleep, I often light a candle briefly at night. It's a personally meaningful time for me to remember why I'm here, a time to join myself with the Divine by whatever name, to step back from the day and take a breath that allows images of quiet into my mind and heart. I am reminded that fire is something that human beings have shared for millennia. For thousands and thousands of years, people of our planet have looked into the center of this life-giving element and experienced a sense of wonder at its warmth and light. This simple practice makes me feel united with a greater whole with a growing and expanding consciousness.

Reflections

Although we do not need a set place to do our mental healing work, it can feel really special when we have one.

Look around and brainstorm places where you might do most of your inner mind work. How might you set up your space?

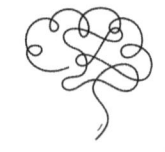

Chapter 16

Why Relax?

NONE OF US can get far if our minds and bodies go in different directions. The best way to bring them together is to breathe deeply and relax.

Our realization of the importance of relaxation is evidenced by a developing branch of medicine dealing with this mind and body state. Being relaxed doesn't mean being sleepy; it just means freeing the body and mind from unnecessary tensions and distractions, allowing them to quiet down and enter a state of balance, creating a positive effect.

In the classic book *The Relaxation Response*, Dr. Herbert Benson of Harvard Medical School points out that relaxation benefits both the mind and the body and that relaxing one tends to relax the other. As our minds quiet down, our bodies relax more. As our bodies relax more, our minds become calmer. The point of relaxation is to ease tension and quiet the action in both our bodies and minds so that the more subtle forms of thinking can occur. There are many ways this can be done.

Breathing is the physical technique used most often to help us relax.

Relaxation takes place naturally as we pay attention to our breath flowing in and out, in and out. Try it now. As you inhale, let the breath travel down into your abdomen rather than stay in the chest area as it usually does. Hold it for a few seconds, slowly releasing the air in a long, steady stream. Repeat this slow abdominal breathing three to five times and feel how your body naturally begins to release tension stored in the muscles. Feel the stress flowing out of your body on the exhalation.

This technique can be practiced anywhere, at any time, to release stored-up tension. By now, it is no secret that medical science believes that much of our illness and disease is caused by the constant tension we store in our bodies. We still react to stressful situations with our early ancestors' adrenaline-pumping "flight or fight" response. They could use all that adrenaline to either kill or run away from a mastodon, but we can't do either if we're sitting in gridlocked traffic. Each time we consciously relax with this simple breathing exercise, we de-tense our bodies and minds and actively do something to become more relaxed, calmer, and healthier.

This relaxed state shifts our attention from the outer world to our inner world. It restores our physiological and psychological balance, allowing us to rest.

We might tell a child who wants to tell us a story, "Wait until I can sit down and listen to you." Similarly, we must take time to sit down to listen as we relax our bodies and minds. As we quiet, the thought chatter slows, and we begin to feel more at peace with ourselves and the world.

In this alert, wakeful but restful state of relaxation, we are most open to receiving new thoughts and developing images in a way that we are not when we are more active and responding to outside pressures. All our attention is focused inward. Our eyes are usually closed, we aren't moving around doing things, and we are centered on the imaginative and feeling parts of ourselves. This is the place of power in which our images have the most significant ability to affect our lives.

The Inner Voice

An inner voice symbolically represents the thought whisperings we can hear when we sit quietly and focus on our thoughts and feelings. These thoughts and feelings spring from deep within ourselves rather than in reaction to outside events in our lives. They come from our center. A quiet voice is just that . . . it is quiet. We rarely hear it when we are busy hurrying about.

The intuitive voice takes many forms, from a flash of insight or a gut-level hunch to full-blown confidence that *this* is what we should be doing. It is that part of us that sees and feels the whole situation and response from that higher level of awareness.

The intuitive sense signals our deepest inclinations
from within, with a feeling of "That's the right thing
for me to do" or "Yes, this is what I want to do."

Unlike your rational, left-brain consciousness—which responds to all the outside "shoulds"—your intuitive sense is in touch with "emotional literacy": the awareness of your deepest feelings and desires about how you can uniquely live your life. Your intuitive sense is your sense of direction—a soul tool. When you use your quiet time to connect with this inner sense, you can recognize your values and make them a reality.

When you follow your intuition, you become a pioneer.

You are venturing into the unknown, the uncharted waters of your psyche, endeavoring to follow your inner guidance rather than relying on what others may be telling you about what you should be doing.

It is transformative to relate to intuition when you express yourself in an artistic work. For a few years, I took classes in my art field and did some fine work, yet only when I listened to my intuitive voice—which encouraged me to work on my own for a year or so without taking classes or instruction—was I able to shed outside influence and develop my unique style of work. It takes courage to "go off by yourself and listen within," but it is worth the journey.

When we heed that inner sense, we may discover that long-sought-after solutions suddenly and spontaneously spring to mind. We have moved from one mode of thinking to another—a more profound, almost mysterious sense of thinking. These answers may come right after focusing intensely on them in our conscious, thinking mind and finally letting them go. You will know when your intuitive voice speaks to you: it is quiet and gentle rather than loud and pushy, and it contains a gem of wisdom you may have missed before.

A central theme of the Mind Fitness philosophy is establishing specific times when we stop all our other activities and change our focus on internal quiet through relaxation.

Reflections

Breathe into your abdomen. Hold your breath for a few seconds before slowly releasing the air in a long, steady stream.

Feel how your body naturally begins to release hidden tensions stored in your muscles.

Feel the stress flowing out of your body with each exhalation.

Allow your mind to rest in the quiet. Do nothing. Just stop.

Chapter 17

A Relaxation Story

THIS IS A story people have found helpful for relaxation. It is a good tool, especially if you record it slowly to play it back to yourself. We all have our ways of finding that relaxed state, and this may serve as a guide.

I am taking the time to sit down and relax now because I know it is good for me. It's something that not only brings me pleasure and peace of mind but is also very good for my body. I quiet my mind, my breathing becomes deeper and fuller, my heart beats slower, and I can feel my muscles loosening, reaching a place of quiet and ease.

I am taking this quiet time each day to improve my health and well-being and welcome new thoughts and feelings that benefit me. This is when I can fill my mind with thoughts of the fullness of my dreams and intentions for myself. This is when my mind can rest in the quietness that brings insight and creative thoughts—as pictures, sensations, or words.

As I take a deep breath, I feel the flood of quietness reach every part of my body. I imagine a golden, honey-colored light pouring down through the top of my head. I feel release as the light touches my eyes, melting all the tension down my cheeks and through my mouth, throat, and neck, inviting me to give in to its warmth and release the tightness in my shoulders, arms, wrists, and fingertips.

I draw in another deep and full breath, shifting the breathing from my chest to my lower abdomen. I breathe again deeply, momentarily hold the air in my stomach, and slowly release it. I feel the richness of the quiet moment alive within me. I allow the quieting to move through my chest, back, stomach, and lower intestines, down through my groin, legs, and feet—relaxing, letting go of all tensions.

I feel the increased oxygen circulating through my brain as I take another deep breath. I call on the power of my concentrated mind to focus on one thing and hold that point for as long as possible. I will focus on an image of a quiet pond with a large full tree standing on its shore, with cattails and other reeds growing around it. The pond is serene and peaceful. There are no ripples on its surface. I soften the light and inhale a sweet scent as I fill my mind with images of this pond. I let go of other thoughts, focusing on the tranquility of mind and body relaxation.

I know that as I focus on the pond and its stillness, my mind will stop whirling around and come to rest in the center of me, providing me with a rest so that I can accomplish all my needs better and faster after my relaxation and peace.

I take in another deep breath and let go of any tensions my body may still be holding as I reflect once again on the pond and its quietness—the beauty of the water's reflection, the fullness of the green tree, and the gentleness of the reeds as they grow near the water's edge.

The image of my relaxed body is a sleeping cat, totally at peace with the world, purring in its most contented way, with no tight muscle anywhere. My body becomes like a cat's—loose, limp, totally at one with the world around me. My body feels heavy as I release any desire to move.

From this quiet place within my mind and body, I experience an inner feeling rising into my awareness of wholeness, beauty, and total tranquility. I feel that bubble of spirit rise, giving new meaning to everything I had been worried about during the day. This clear bubble that I imagine is a spiritual essence within me that unites my body, mind, and heart.

In this place of quietness, I ask for thoughts about how to live my life, solve my problems, and be supportive of others. I take another deep breath, knowing I have taken quiet time to nourish myself and connect my body and spirit. I know that my body heals itself, that my mind reaches a point of clarity, and that my spirit touches the source of life.

I feel myself awakening to the reality around me. I wiggle my fingers and toes, take a deep breath, slowly open my eyes, and feel refreshed and unified in body, mind, and heart, knowing I did something good for myself today.

Reflections

Read this chapter slowly to yourself and record yourself reading, then play it back to yourself. Better yet, have someone else read it to you while you do the relaxing!

How does it feel to allow yourself to simply relax for your own well-being?

Chapter 18

In Your Mind's Eye
Visualize

Visualization means using the mind's eye to picture a desired intention. When we visualize, we create an experience with our imaginations, using as many senses as possible: sight, hearing, touch, smell, and taste. The result can be more positive attitudes and states of mind, a good grade on a test, an athletic performance, healing from an illness—quite literally, anything we can imagine.

Imaging is the very core of the active part of Mind Fitness training. It is essential to change any habit or learn any new skill. We must be able to imagine the change to create it.

> *Carl Jung wrote, "But what great thing came into existence that was not first fantasy? All the works of humanity have their origin in creative imagination. . . Fantasy is a natural and vital activity which helps the seeds of development to grow."*

Anything we create has to exist first in our minds. We can't create or change anything unless we can imagine it first. Imagining ourselves functioning optimally helps us to be that way. The activity comes to life mentally first.

We move from vague, abstract desires to more concrete planning by creating mental pictures and feelings of our goals. This translation from abstract to concrete gives the Mind Fitness process its power.

One thing that makes visualization so effective is that it uses part of the mind-brain system in which mental images are born. In Western society, we are trained to use our analytical, logical, language-oriented mind-brain systems, so this focus on the imaginative function represents a shift.

We must gently urge ourselves away from the predominantly rational, spoken-word world and refocus our attention on the more diffuse and subtle energies that make up our imagination.

We may feel silly at first, sitting with our eyes closed and calling up images of how we would like our lives to be and how we would like to feel. We've been cautioned about "daydreaming" and never been taught that it's all right—much less desirable—to spend time each day "doing nothing." By "doing nothing," we are taking an active role in creating our futures. However, times are changing, and new research in the field of biopsychology—the interplay between the mind and body—is growing. Rollo May emphasizes this changing perception when he asks:

> *"What if imagination and art were not the frosting at all,*
> *but the fountainhead of human experience?"*

As we permit ourselves to drift in that intuitive, creative, nonlinear, right-brain part of ourselves, we begin to feel more comfortable and receptive there. We begin to touch a new spiritual part of our human experience. Now, we can draw mental pictures and feelings from that right brain that will focus us on how we want to be.

Mind and Body

Visualization not only enhances memory and creativity but also improves physical performance. When we imagine ourselves acting, such as playing tennis, the picture in our mind fires the brain's neurons to activate the muscles we would use in that activity. As we imagine the perfect tennis stroke, tiny impulses are sent to the exact muscles we would use to make that motion. It's as if we physically took the swing in miniature. We may feel the muscle twitch or feel nothing, but our body has established a pattern, duplicating that perfect tennis stroke.

> *When we repeat the images, the pattern continues*
> *to build between the mind and body.*

When we get out on the tennis court, our stroke has improved. We have practiced it with our minds and bodies without ever leaving the house.

The same principle holds for all physical activities. That is why watching a video of a perfect golf swing with active attention will improve one's golf game.

Using all the Senses

Visualization is partially a misnomer because we don't just use our visual sense. The more senses we can involve in our imaging, the better—hearing, seeing, feeling, smelling, tasting, and combining different senses. The goal is to create the illusion of actually being there, doing the activity, or existing in the state of mind that we imagine.

Imaging or visualizing isn't just thinking about something. There is a difference between thinking and imaging. Imaging means *involvement* in the activity—allowing ourselves to feel the emotions, heightening the physical sensations, and making them as natural as possible—being mentally proactive. The most potent images are vivid, involving all the senses and bringing emotions into play. We can call it mind painting. The mind becomes a canvas on which we experiment with painting and sensing various forms and colors. The broader our range of colors and senses, the greater our possibilities.

Passionate Energy

Visualizing is an *active* process. Imaging doesn't just happen to us; it takes personal motivation and a solid commitment to ourselves. We must *do something*. Whether we want to heal our unloving thinking patterns, lose five pounds, hit a baseball better, close a business deal, or pass a test, we must commit clear, vital energy to our goal.

Winners in all fields share one characteristic:
passion for their goals.

They are so involved with what they are doing that they visualize their goals without thinking about them. That's just where their minds naturally gravitate. The successful teacher plans and thinks about her students; the tennis player or gymnast visualizes the perfect strokes and acrobatics; the painter visualizes his next creation; the pregnant woman is absorbed in thoughts about loving a healthy, happy baby.

These people visualize and experience the desired results on deep mental and emotional levels. They *live* their visualizations, even driving along the freeway or sitting in a movie theater when the images occur. They are positively obsessed with their visions, so they spend a lot of time living the experiences of success in their minds' eyes.

We can do the same thing with personal negative thinking patterns. It's hard to get positively excited about obsessive, hostile thoughts. Until now, we may have been in the habit of obsessing about negative things, concentrating all our energy, dreams, and images on what was *wrong*.

> *The key here is to focus not on the negativity*
> *but on the constructive feelings and behaviors*
> *we want to create in our moment-to-moment lives.*

Until now, you may have been pulled unknowingly into a habit of obsessing about the worst possibilities, concentrating your energy, dreams, and images on what was wrong. Your mind has gravitated toward the negative. Now, let's at least give those automatic thoughts some competition! To do that, we want to actively visualize something we *can* get excited about—a more loving and nurturing way of relating to ourselves, a stronger self-image as it relates to what we want to do with our lives, and deeper, more intimate relationships. Let's take the focus off of the external and what we judge as not correct.

> *We want to become proactive and directive in turning a*
> *recognized negative attitude into something more empowering.*

Whenever we get lost in negative ideas, daydreaming about our unworthiness, or being a victim, we need to say, "*Stop!*" After we stop, we need to find another, more positive image to replace the old one. We must *step in actively*, stop the automatic thinking pattern, and then take concrete steps to replace it with positive images. It's a self-directed pivot, sometimes even a complete 180 or U-turn, when we find the mind obsessing—replacing that old, worn-out thinking with thoughts we consciously choose. I call it a "stop and about-face." It is a clear change in our thinking. Sometimes it works, sometimes it doesn't—but at least we are no longer just running on automatic reactions with their endlessly repeated mental cycles. We have a tool to help us move into a thinking pattern that is more empowering and healthful in the long run.

Learning a new habit starts with creating a situation in our minds and hearts. We must see the new behavior in our mind before we can demonstrate and live it.

Several months after Jim began his proactive reflections, he still found himself worrying compulsively about his freelance photography business. He had several regular clients and had been successful for two years, but Jim harbored fears of all his business drying up overnight. He even extended this fantasy to imagining himself as a "bag man" with no money and no place to stay, sleeping in the park.

Jim's friends laughed because he looked so successful, and they couldn't imagine him on the streets, but the fantasy was genuine to him. Although phobias are rarely based on reality, that does not diminish their power over the individual. This vision of poverty was so strong that Jim often felt overwhelmed, powerless to stop it from running repeatedly in his head.

His perseverance and absolute unwillingness to be defeated by a thinking habit finally enabled Jim to conquer his automatic negative thinking. He made a decision. Each time a fearful fantasy rose in his mind, he stopped whatever he was doing and devoted all of his energy to handling that negative image. He sat down, closed his eyes, and told it to STOP. Sometimes, it did right away; sometimes, it took a little longer. But Jim never gave up. He kept at it, and gradually, he had more and more success, making the old habitual fantasy shut down. Eventually, he consciously replaced his negative thoughts with his vision of what he called "The Other Side."

In this image, all the fear of failure was gone. Jim had gotten to The Other Side of his negative mental habits and was living a life free from worry about business and money. In his imagination, he saw himself shooting pictures in the Himalayas, in Africa, in Japan—all the places he most wanted to visit—and being paid more money than he knew what to do with. He used the same images each time so that they could grow stronger and stronger within him. He let himself *feel* the success and absorbed those emotions deep within himself. He tasted the exotic foods, smelled the strange, pungent odors of those exciting places, felt the ground under his feet, and saw how the sun shone differently in various places worldwide.

The stronger his images of The Other Side became, the more they eclipsed his old, negative fantasies, which were pretty shopworn and not nearly as exciting.

No one else can heal the automatic fear-ridden thoughts that make up the various forms of the disease of negativity for each of us. It's entirely in our hands. As we develop a passionate commitment and desire to kick the habit of automatic fearful thinking, we know that more enlightening thoughts will follow.

Remember that for many of us, with our backgrounds of early hurts, loving ourselves is not an automatic response but a learned skill.

Reflections

Begin to imagine yourself living to your fullest. Breathe.

Chapter 19

It's All Yours!

A Personal Program

Each of us must take an individualized approach to our Mind Fitness. Only we know what makes us peaceful, relaxed, and fulfilled—and those things will likely differ for each of us. The images we develop from our creative imaginations will be specifically designed to take each of us where we want to go.

Some of us will start by focusing on a better relationship with our children or spouse. Others will want a more positive attitude in business. Others will need a fuller and more rewarding personal life, more friends, and some new creative projects. Some of us will want to stop feeling so tired, irritable, moody, and pressured all the time. Some will be thinking about dramatic life changes. Others won't want to alter anything but will want to see and experience everything from a more balanced and optimistic point of view.

> *Since we are the only ones who know what makes us*
> *feel balanced and fulfilled, it's vital to give some*
> *attention to what creates that feeling.*

When I pose this question in workshops, a surprising number of people draw a blank. We're not taught to think about what would make us happy, and very few of us do. We mull over what makes us *un*happy—and we can often pinpoint what's *wrong* in our lives, making long lists of problems—but very few of us actually sit down and think specifically about the things that would make us feel love and happiness.

Make a list of things that make your life happy.
Close your eyes and get a perfect image of your life and feelings
if you were filled with love and completely happy.

It can be seeing a sunset, walking in the Autumn leaves, crushing them under your feet, or taking a warm bath. These are little things to become aware of. Can you list twenty such little moments?

One woman did this in a workshop and found herself imagining the same attitudes, actions, and behaviors she already had in her life. To her surprise, she was happy as she was! "I discovered that I have been happy and successful all my life," she said, "and I never even knew it!" She changed her self-definition accordingly. Most of us will find that we want to make some changes, but we may also be surprised at how many aspects of our reality resemble our ideal.

Creating the Picture

There are different kinds of imagery: Memory Images, Creative Images, Intuitive Images, and Purposeful Creative Images. Let's look quickly at each.

Memory Images are pictures from the past, such as where and how things are. We use images from our daily memory—to drive to that restaurant where we dined last year, to locate that library book we must return, and so on. We recall the pattern of the streets we went through; we remember where we tend to stash things temporarily in the house. We use memory images when we recall the view from our bedroom window, the sound of someone's voice, or the smell of bread baking in the oven.

The danger inherent in Memory Images is that we can get into the habit of going through day after day using *only* memory, reactivating the same emotions without stopping to consider whether we want them, without remembering that we have it in our power to create new feelings and beliefs. When we fall into the old, self-defeating, pessimistic habits of thought, we rely only on obsessive memory patterns of thinking. This leaves us playing the same old emotional tapes without creating new ones more fitting, perhaps, for today's reality.

This is not to say that images from the past are not helpful: We need them to negotiate in the world, to get from one place to another, and to remember how to use the washing machine. They are the guiding threads of our days. However, we don't want to function primarily from memory rather than giving each fresh experience its due. We are in trouble once we start operating only from the past—especially using memories that promote our version of negativity.

Creative Images are new thoughts—things we've never thought of in precisely that way; new perceptions and beliefs about ourselves and others. Creative Images come from releasing old memories and images of the past, from forgiving others and ourselves. Creative Images call on the imagination to paint new pictures in our minds. Creating an image takes a little more energy than replaying the same old pictures, but the rewards are worth the extra effort. By activating our imaginations and giving them free rein regularly, we can begin to draw ourselves the way we would like to be, imagine the activities that would bring us the most pleasure, and let ourselves feel the emotions that make us feel most alive.

Joseph Campbell, the well-known mythologist, calls this process "Following your bliss." It is the essence of a self-actualized, fully living, and loving person.

Now let's look at two kinds of Creative Images: Intuitive and Purposeful. Purposeful Images are self-directed, like arrows toward a specific, well-defined goal. I'll discuss these in the next section, focusing first on Intuitive Images.

Intuitive Images are not so tightly defined as Purposeful Images; we let them bubble up from our intuition. With Intuitive Imaging, we come to our quiet time with no specific goal and allow our inner voices to rise to the surface at their own will and speak to us. When we clear the mind and wait quietly for intuitive images or sensations, a particular thought, idea, or feeling that is more insightful than anything we might have thought with our conscious minds may float to the surface.

*Sometimes, the unconscious has some surprising
things to say. More often than not, those things
are more important than we thought.*

Matthew Fox, author and philosopher on creative spirituality, says that
"wisdom requires imagination and nurtures it." He's talking about a
coming together of the whole: conscious and unconscious, inner and
outer awareness. The quiet part of Mind Fitness encourages such a
joining and unity.

At one seminar, Steve described being unhappy about not having a
special woman in his life. The rest of his life was going very well: His
career as an engineer took off, there were no financial worries, and he
had many friends. Yet somehow, having a successful relationship had
eluded him. This was the area where he concentrated his Mind Fitness
program. He had done purposeful imaging on the subject, clarifying
his values and what he wanted in a relationship. He had asked himself
questions. Now, he decided to supplement his idealized versions with
some Intuitive Images.

But when Steve sat down, cleared his mind, relaxed his body, and began
opening up to whatever Intuitive Images came his way, all he could see
was an image of himself playing racquetball. He had played a lot of
racquetball several years earlier when it had been fashionable. But then
his career had become more time-consuming, and he had gotten involved
in bicycling; he hadn't played racquetball since and had no conscious
desire to do so.

Steve let the image go, took another deep breath, and cleared his
mind. Again, the picture of himself playing racquetball floated to the
surface. He gave up on Intuitive Imaging for the afternoon but later
thought playing a few racquetball games might be fun. He called his old
racquetball partner, Rob, and persuaded him to take a couple of hours off
on Saturday afternoon for old-time's sake.

They had a good game, and afterward, they met a woman named Eileen
in the juice bar. Steve has been seeing her ever since.

Images with a Purpose

Purposeful Creative Images are specifically designed to make something happen. Sometimes, people find this a bit intimidating; they fear they "won't be able to come up with any good images" or will "freeze up" when asked to let something entirely new come into their minds. But almost everyone finds the process surprisingly easy with just a little practice. It's as old as "wishing on a star."

First, relax. Take a few deep breaths and let all the tension pour out of your body. Now, consciously tell yourself that you will visualize yourself doing something you would like to be doing. To get used to this, start with something you've done before rather than a completely new activity. When you have the picture in your mind, begin filling in more details and making the picture as vivid as possible.

Suppose, for instance, you create the image of walking on the beach. Imagine your feet on the warm sand as you walk along, enjoying the sound of the waves, the sight of the blue sky, and the smell of the seaweed washing up along the shore. Taste the salt in the air as the sea breezes touch your face and arms. Let these sensations create awareness of joy and pleasure, bubbling up inside as you spread your arms to embrace this moment.

Try this exercise with some other activities you've already experienced, then move on to creating new experiences.

Remember, visualization works best when all the
senses are brought into play and you give
yourself emotionally to the experience.

The more details you can include, the better. The more thoroughly you can experience the mental and emotional conditions you imagine, the more influential the imaging will be. It's like "mind drawing," using all of the senses, making your intention very clear to yourself. This helps you recognize it when it comes your way.

One of my first experiences with Purposeful Creative Imagery happened when our rented house was sold, and we had to move. I decided to imagine the new home we would find. I took a few relaxing breaths and visualized the house as if I were drawing it.

The kind of house I wanted surfaced immediately in my mind's eye. I saw it bathed in sunshine, near town, on a relatively flat street that allowed bike riding. I went for the ideal as I mentally drew the living room with a lot of glass and heard the sound of birds singing outside.

Several times a day, I made a point of flashing that picture in my mind's eye. I approached it each time with total assurance, not allowing any doubts to occupy my mind. I did not permit any negative thoughts that might have made me pessimistic—like that most of the town was hilly and had large redwood trees that shaded most homes. I held steadfastly to the picture I'd created in my mind—as I stepped out of the shower, waited at a stop light, stood in line to buy cat food, and walked across a room. I flashed on the image as often as I remembered to do so.

Sure enough, within a few months, we were living in a home very much like the one I had imagined. When we define and get clear on what we want, we are more likely to have it come our way. It may be that we recognize it.

Mind Lifts Means Pumping Images

My constant, regular flashing of the image of our ideal new home was one of my most effortless—and effective—experiences of frequent imaging. I kept thinking about it naturally and could easily visualize what we wanted. You can think of these short flashes—brief visions of positive images— like sets of lifting weights or pumping iron, except it's your imagination doing the lifting. I call it Pumping Images or Mind Lifts.

You can create your Mind Lifts and pump whatever images you wish. Here are two for generally "pumping up" self-esteem and confidence.

- *Imagine yourself giving a speech, a presentation, or even a dinner. Instead of concentrating on your familiar fears, start to see yourself standing up in front of the group with confidence and enthusiasm. See the size and shape of the room, the kinds of chairs people sit in, and the people in the audience. Sense the taste in your mouth, the smells in the room, the sound of applause, and the emotional excitement of making your presentation. Image things precisely as you would like them to be, and know that as you do this, you carry the benefits and sense of accomplishment into every area of your life.*

- *Suppose that you would like to have a more exciting job. Imagine exactly what that job would look like. Remember, you are pretending, so make it as ideal as you can. What specific activities are you doing? What are you wearing? How does the work feel? With whom are you working? See the colors of your new surroundings, sense the sounds, the smells, and the general atmosphere of the new workplace. See yourself talking with your boss and hearing her praise you for your fine work. Feel your hand in a handshake as you are congratulated for your outstanding contribution. Feel a sense of emotional abundance and wholeness within yourself. Know that anything you can imagine, you can achieve.*

Reflections

Continue to create meaningful images for self-empowerment.

Chapter 20

Why Affirm?

Affirmations are clear statements that the realities we want are possible. They are declarations of possibility and trust.

Here are some examples of affirmations people have created in seminars. These statements help guide their thinking in the direction they want. Participants drew strength and clarity of intention from these personal directives:

- I am learning to say "Yes!"
- I have been successful in my life.
- I believe in and trust myself.
- I am loving myself and others more and more.
- I choose to heal my negative patterns and think supportive, constructive thoughts.
- I accept and forgive myself.
- I am a peaceful, committed person.

Affirmations seem so simple that people sometimes dismiss them as self-deluding chatter that merely works like a placebo—making us feel better but having no actual effect on reality. People who have fallen prey to the cynical, pessimistic, "guilty until proven innocent" mentality are particularly apt to put down affirmations. Some of this comes from the indoctrination we've all received that tells us that anything so simple yet so untouchable and not statistically measurable has to be stupid.

However, when we understand the power of verbal thinking, we realize that talking to ourselves, whether in affirming or disrespecting terms, plays a crucial role in our mental well-being. Our self-definition and the declarations we make to ourselves are important.

Affirmations have astonishing power, especially when consciously incorporated with images. Linear, left-brain, language-based affirmations are a powerful complement to intuitive, right-brain, picture-based images.

Belief in Ourselves

Trust and belief in ourselves are essential to good mental health. Affirmations reinforce the faith that we can reach our goals and believe in ourselves. They guide our behavior by reminding us of what we value and how we want to be in our lives. By being proactive, we put awareness and thought into our affirmations. We can't just mouth the words and hope for the best; putting the intentional power of our attention, will, and feelings behind them is essential.

We can all tell the difference between an actor simply reading the script and someone who puts feeling and emotional energy into what she is saying. The words delivered with emotion create a spark of feeling within us—sometimes so strong that we have physical reactions, such as tensing our muscles, laughing, or crying. The intention and the active emotional energy behind an affirmation make it robust.

If, for some reason, we find it hard to believe what we're saying in an affirmation, we can stop and examine what specific doubt is undercutting that belief. The important thing is to be aware of our reactions and notice when doubts prevent us from getting behind our beliefs. For instance, if we find ourselves wincing each time we say, "I deserve a job I love," we can stop for a moment and look for the source of that reaction. What is undercutting our belief that we deserve a job we love? We might have bought something our parents said long ago about work being a struggle, not an enjoyable activity. Or we might have been told we'd never get a job we liked without certain educational degrees.

Once we know the barrier, we can examine it and let it go. It's not true that work has to be drudgery, and once we understand that we've been holding this false belief in our unconscious, we can forgive ourselves and let it go. It's not true that we need certain degrees to enjoy our work, but we might never even have realized that we held that unconscious belief if we hadn't brought it to the surface through examination with affirmations.

> *Through affirmations, we create the reality in*
> *our minds before our intention happens.*

The more deeply we believe in our ability to reach our goals, the more likely we are to do so. Affirmations guide our perceptions and put us into the "*I can*" mode of thinking.

Willis Harmon wrote in *Higher Creativity,* "Affirmation is a way of reprogramming the unconscious idea and image processor through mental and vocal repetition of the ideas or images which we want our minds to accept as 'input.'" We may want to try reprogramming to make these changes:

- Create more positive attitudes.
- Experience more self-confidence and trust.
- Improve our relationships with family and coworkers.
- Develop a new relationship.
- Make more money.
- Experience more passion in life.
- Feel more empowered and personally secure.
- Work up the courage to make a career change.
- Perform a job or sport with more competence.

We've been concentrating on connecting with the purposeful and intuitive in learning to visualize. Affirmations translate our creative images into meaningful words. We are language-based beings and need to include language in our learning; affirmations reinforce in words the belief that we can do whatever we are visualizing.

Affirmations also allow us to retrieve images from our unconscious. Language is composed of symbols we use to organize things in our minds. If we want to call up something from our unconscious, we'll have more luck if it has a name. We might say, for instance, "It's time for my relaxation period. I think I'll call up that image I used last time of the pond with the reeds and the glass-like surface." This brings back the meditation we used last time and gives us access to that part of our unconscious. Words help us proactively guide our thinking patterns. They narrate the story and strongly direct our tone and mood. They form an essential part of our attitude, whether positive or negative.

With affirmations, we use language to help us move to images—guiding our thinking with the words. To test this, imagine an apple *without* saying "apple" in your mind. We use words to label the memory files in our minds for fast, easy retrieval. Affirmations form the bridge between our inner world of visualization and the outer world of physical reality. When we pair word power with emotional feeling and sensory images, we have a tremendously potent force that galvanizes our intentions and ability to create in the world.

To define is to create.

Reflections

Now it is time to add declarations of intent to your visualized goals. Create one or two affirmations for yourself that carry your strong emotional intentions.

Grant them more power by writing and repeating them several times a day.

Yes, you can do this!

Chapter 21

It's for You!
Make the Words Your Own

It's POWERFUL TO repeat affirmations regularly, just as it is important to return again and again to the mental images empowering us. We want to *own* these images and words. Research shows that specific thoughts produce physical changes in our bodies, brains, chemistry, and muscles. Actual physical connections are made among various parts of the brain and between the brain and the body. The internal structure of our brains is constantly changing, depending on what we are doing, experiencing, or thinking. Each time we repeat a thought pattern, the brain's neural structure physically changes. Here's how it works:

Our brains are made up of billions of interconnecting neural fibers. The places where these fibers connect are called *synapses.* At each synapse, the electrical impulse generated by the thought has to jump from one piece of neural fiber to the next. Amazingly, each time we think a thought, there is a slight modification in that synapse. It's as if a minor "groove" is started, and the next time we think that same thought, it is easier for the neural impulse to make that same jump again.

Recent research shows that the brain is continually modifying itself. That is the Up Side: we can learn new ways of thinking and being! When patterns are repeated, the neural pathways form deeper "grooves" that make the jump easier and more accessible. That's how we learn to do things automatically. The first time we play a piano piece, we may hesitate and halt our movements, but after repeated practice, we can play it "without thinking." In the same way, we hit a tennis ball so often over the years that the motion becomes "automatic."

These grooves may make it challenging to break negative habits, but their presence shows us that we can create new grooves and new habits at any time in life. In *The Brain Book*, Peter Russell says, "Learning almost always results in some of the brain's trillions of synapses changing their ability to transmit impulses." That means that the more we do or say something, the more our brains change to accommodate that new pattern of thinking or action. This is the process by which affirmations change not only our thoughts but the actual structure of our brains!

In our eagerness to succeed and move forward,
it is sometimes tempting to change directives too quickly.

If we don't get results within twenty-four hours, we switch to another set of words. Sometimes, the process of making new thoughts of our own takes time. If you don't feel good about an affirmation, by all means, move on to something else. But it's also essential to give a new affirmation some time to settle in and allow the new "grooves" to form. Choose the affirmations you want and stick to those for a month or so. Allow each new mindset to work with your images and pump some feeling into them.

Try turning off the car radio when you drive and using that time to do affirmations. Some people record a few affirmations to play while driving or walking, leaving about ten seconds between each one so that they can say them aloud. You can affirm silently in the line at the market, walking down the street, doing the dishes, whenever you have some down mental time that you want to enjoy more and put to good use! This keeps your mind chatter in the direction you want to go.

Worded in the Positive

Affirmations are more accessible for the mind to digest and act on if they are phrased positively. We always get better results when we ask a child (or anyone) to *do* something than when we tell them *not* to do something.

If we create negatively stated affirmations, we force our minds to shift into reverse and find a behavior opposite to what is said in the affirmation rather than following the more direct route of simply doing as it is told. For example, "I don't want to be sick any longer" is not the same clear directive as *"I am focused on being healthy."*

Positively phrased affirmations also leave less room for doubt about what we want. They represent the difference between saying, "I'll try to meet you if I can make it," and "I will be there." We say, *"This* is what I want," rather than, "Well, I'm not sure what I want, but I know I don't want *that."*

How to Create Powerful Affirmations

The best affirmations are those that captivate your imagination. They arise from the true desires you have discovered through your intuitive sensing and different forms of visualizations.

Word in the first person, present tense. Using the first-person "I" makes affirmations our own. And even when we're not experiencing a great sense of well-being, we need to word affirmations in the present tense. Here are a couple examples and reminders:

- "I am a happy and secure person." (*Not* "I *will be* a happy and secure person." or "It's good to be happy and secure.")
- "I am ready for the perfect relationship." (*Not* "I will be ready for the perfect relationship when it comes along." or "It would be great to have a perfect relationship.")
- **Reinforce with positive feelings and emotions.** If you affirm that you are wealthy, well-known for your creative talents, or in excellent health, use your imagination to experience exactly how you think that would feel. See your life as that of a very talented person who is respected for their work or who exudes health. See your surroundings under these circumstances and concentrate on the feelings you would have. Keep it somewhat reality based.
- **Believe without question.** If you doubt what you are affirming, use it as an opportunity to discover and deflate that doubt.

Then, return to trusting and knowing that what you assert is ideally possible.

- **Repeat regularly and often.** This can be done in a concentrated period of Mind Fitness exercising as you walk, wait in line, hold on the telephone, or whenever you think of it during the day.
- **State clearly and positively.** Instead of "I will not eat any fattening foods today," try "Today I am choosing to eat only healthy, slimming foods." This is a more explicit message to the mind and concentrates on attaining a positive result rather than avoiding a negative one. It also eliminates the possibility that the mind might not catch that little "not" in the sentence and misinterpret it—for example, "I will not smoke" as "I will smoke."

Life-Affirming Words of Intention

Even when we are not working on any specific issue, we can direct our energy into thoughts of good health and optimistic attitudes by focusing on general statements of well-being. These sentences are self-directives, reminding us of how we want to be.

For Good Health
- I am strong, flexible, and healthy.
- I give thanks for being in good health.
- My body and I are friends, and I want to take care of my body.
- I relax my body and mind by taking a deep breath.
- I choose healthy things to optimize my health.

For Emotional Well-Being
- I remain centered and calm.
- I am relaxed and at ease.
- I value being a humorous person.
- I respond to others with loving compassion.
- My emotions are excellent guides for me.
- I keep my positive feelings out front as much as possible.

For the Intellect
- I am open to new things.
- I grasp new information quickly and respond appropriately.

- I welcome the higher wisdom that flows into me.
- I am flexible and creative in my thinking.
- I have unexpected creative thoughts that are strokes of genius.
- The most amazingly profitable thoughts come into my mind.

For Spiritual Growth

- I am one with others. I know and embrace that part of me larger than my personality or physical form.
- I am part of the expanding life force, the highest good I can imagine.
- I am a trusting, loving, and loved person. I feel peaceful in myself. I smile to myself in gratitude.
- I am comforted as I join with others who share this earth. I affirm my human family.
- I feel the gentleness of Divine love sweeping through me.

Shaping Reality

Words carry power. This is an important theme that runs through Mind Fitness. When we consciously engage our minds in repeating affirmations, we take charge of what our minds say to our bodies. The process of affirming brings all the parts of us together—mind, body, brain, heart, and spirit—and lets them function as an integrated whole. This is a tremendously empowering process.

We are learning that our beliefs create what we think of as reality, and we only perceive the things we believe in. It is challenging to see something we cannot consider real, even if it is right before us. If we saw a unicorn on the way to work, our first thought would probably *not* be, "Gee, and all this time, I thought that unicorns didn't exist! I must have been wrong." Our first thought would probably be that someone was trying to trick us by attaching a fake horn to a miniature horse or that we must be seeing things.

So, we perceive what we can believe in or expect to perceive—the things in our "belief set." Consciously choosing which affirmations we want to repeat to ourselves is one way of expanding our belief sets to include more successful perceptions of ourselves and our situations.

If we repeat six times a day for a month, "People want to support me. No one is out to get me. Most people only want to do things that will be supportive of me," this may alter our perception of how people relate to us. The synapses will be changed, how we think about ourselves will be expanded, and how we think about and respond to others will be transformed.

One of our seminar participants wanted to think more positively about what she *did* have in her life rather than constantly dwelling on what she *didn't* have in her life and how unhappy she was. She decided on the affirmation, "I have everything I need to be happy now."

After a month, she returned to the group to report that something extraordinary had happened. On the fifth day of guiding her thinking with this affirmation, she began to notice things that had been in her life all along but that she had never perceived as contributing to her happiness. She began appreciating her wonderful house, her cat's affection, and many friends. Not only did she realize that she was much happier than she'd thought, but she noticed more positive things and people were coming into her life. She began to think of affirmations as magnets, which is precisely how they work.

Reflections

Use the affirmations offered and create your images.

See and feel the affirmation as you say it. Breathe. Feel. Repeat.

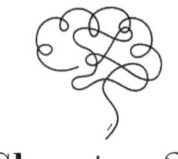

Chapter 22

What's the Timing?
Rhythm and Style

T HERE IS ANOTHER element to Mind Fitness that is equally as important as relaxation, visualization, and affirmation. It is rhythm and style—that is, being in harmony with various activities' inherent rhythms and with our own personal rhythms and styles.

Personal Rhythm

We all have our own individual energy patterns and learning styles as we operate in the world. Some of us are more outgoing, assertive, and independent; others are more internal, calm, and collaborative. Some of us are auditory; others are visual or tactile learners. Some of us are morning people; others are night people. Some like to move in and assess a situation immediately; others like to "wait and see." Some need to nap in the afternoon; others require only a few hours of sleep each night— some of us like a faster pace in life, and others a slower one.

We all have a sense of our internal patterns.

It's essential to accept and embrace those patterns and incorporate them into a personalized program of Mind Fitness. For example, if you are a morning person and fade fast after 7:00 p.m., you would want to avoid scheduling your inner-mind focusing time in the late evening. If you're a night person and don't come alive until noon, you probably don't want to make your Mind Fitness time 6:00 a.m. The key is finding when it's easiest for you to be both relaxed and alert so you can bring your best to your Mind Fitness session.

We want to create our own rhythms within our Mind Fitness program by using repetitive associations to help us move more quickly and easily into the states of relaxation, inner listening, imaging, and affirming. We can put reinforcement principles to work for us, using certain sounds, smells, and sights to help trigger our inner rhythms.

Some of us reflect best in front of a small altar with incense, candles, and soft music. Others may prefer sitting by the ocean, in the garden, or on the sofa in the living room. We each have our favorite kinds of music. It's not important what our personal rhythms *are*; it's important that we become aware of them and use them to our advantage rather than trying to work against them because they don't "look right" or we have never done it that way before.

Activity Rhythm

This is pretty obvious, but how often it's overlooked is incredible. Each activity also has its inherent natural rhythm. The rhythm of golf is different from the rhythm of basketball. A household project's rhythm and style differs from the rhythm and style needed for a business venture. As we do visualizations and affirmations relating to improving our health or performance in various activities, we need to be conscious of the activity's built-in rhythm and use it to our advantage.

*It's easy to grow discouraged by thinking
something will happen sooner than it will.*

For example, the rhythm of healing from major surgery is very different from that of getting over the flu. If you know the rhythm of healing from the surgery, you are not apt to grow frustrated by the longer time needed for complete recovery. You are expecting it to take longer, and indeed it does. The important thing is that you have consciously considered the activity's rhythm and don't expect it to be different from what it is. If you go to a doctor's appointment expecting it to take fifteen minutes, you will probably experience frustration and stress. Realistically assessing your activity's rhythm cycles and needs is vital to your mental health and peace of mind.

Finding Your Rhythm

You may already have some idea of how you learn best and what kind of environment will help you most as you begin your Mind Fitness Program. We all have different rhythms. We may respond to visual elements and have candles or flowers in the place where we do our Mind Fitness exercises. We may use a scent to trigger mental patterns that put us into the state we want for this relaxing time. We may respond strongly to sounds and want to play the same music each day so that our bodies and minds get used to that rhythm as part of our visualizing and affirming process. Playing the same music during your quieting sessions helps trigger your relaxation responses. We may find that being outdoors is important for our rhythm.

Whatever rhythms we use, the point is to establish our "grooves" so that when we hear that music, smell that fragrance, or see that candle, we go more quickly and comfortably into the open and relaxed state we seek. It boils down to this:

The Mind Fitness session is a daily time that involves relaxing the body and mind and shifting our attention from the outside world inward to where we shape our reality.

These few minutes of quieting for proactive reflection and purposeful imagery *do* actually shape our reality. They guide our perceptions and expand what we are open to experiencing.

Reflections

Take time to notice your own personal rhythms and the timing needed for your activities.

Chapter 23

Prepping for Your "No Sweat" Workout

Are you ready to create your orientation toward full potential and health?

THIS IS SAYING "yes" to our well-being, knowing that our well-being leads to better decisions and actions in the outer world.

The core steps in any Mind Fitness program can be done in a simple seven-step workout that usually takes about twenty minutes. Ideally, you'll do it every day at the same time and place, although you can do it anytime and anywhere. I am a "do it anytime, anywhere" person. This may be closing my eyes at the airport, sitting quietly in my car for a few minutes, or a couple moments of conscious breathing before an appointment.

But I do this in some way as close to every day as I can, which is the secret. You will personalize your program, tailoring it to fit your rhythms and goals, but the seven steps described in the next chapter will still form the ideal foundation—a backbone, if you will—for creating increased peace and health in your life.

As with physical fitness, each person's Mind Fitness workout program is unique. I want to emphasize this:

Each person's approach to their well-being will differ.

So feel free to experiment with your approach to your time-out session. Experiment with various techniques, be creative, and above all, ensure your Mind Fitness workout is rejuvenating, peaceful, and empowering for you.

Work with Your Rhythm

Some people like a more extended relaxation period and take extra time to enjoy that peaceful, serene place within themselves; others relax more quickly and go immediately to their visualizations and affirmations. Some people like a dramatic setting with an altar, flowers, incense, and music; others prefer a more low-key session and are content to sit quietly on the sofa and journey inward. Some people see their Mind Fitness workout as the most dynamic and creative period of their day; others see it as the most restful time. In the last chapter's reflection, you took some time to notice your personal rhythms and the time you need for your Mind Fitness activities.

Choosing the mental and physical environment
and rhythms that work best for you is essential.

As you start doing the program daily, you will adapt your setting as needed to fit your rhythm perfectly. All that's necessary is that you are able to sit comfortably in a chair, on the floor, or somewhere outside in nature.

When you can, work on sitting up straight so that energy can flow all through your body. Sitting up is preferable to lying down—so that you remain alert and relaxed rather than falling asleep—but I do sometimes lie down to do my quieting. There are no rules—get to know what is peaceful for you. Commit to being quiet with yourself each day. Even if all you do is sit down quietly and take five prolonged, conscious, deep breaths, you will feel the healing begin.

Remember these keys to success:
- Set aside time each day for relaxing, visualizing, and affirming.
- Do your exercises as regularly as possible, preferably at the same time each day, but any time is good.

- When possible, create a special place that allows you to remember the greater whole in your life.

If Mind Fitness is so uncomplicated, why does it take practice? Why can't we toss off a ten- to twenty-minute session every week or two to get the same results?

There are three reasons.

First, personal negativity patterns are usually lifelong habits. We have twenty, forty, sixty, or more years of negative training of habits to overcome. It's as if we have spent all those years looking for love in all the wrong places. It takes some doing to break those old habits. We're involved in stopping the momentum in one direction and actively fueling it in another.

Without a regular program of mental reflection and focus that actively steers the mind away from negativity and replaces it with something positive, we tend to gravitate back toward our old, familiar thinking patterns. Left to our own devices, we will see the limited and challenging side of things more often.

Second, if we are focused on feelings of defeat, part of our negative programming may be that we don't deserve a new, positive perspective and all the benefits it will bring. We may be able to visualize the ideal life, job, or relationship, but somewhere in our unconscious, we don't believe that we are entitled to it or are capable of achieving it.

We may even go so far as to sabotage ourselves with self-defeating, negative mind chatter, like "That would be nice, but what have I ever done to deserve it? Even if I got it, I'd just mess it up." or "That's a great job, but they would never hire me."

We don't even have to put these thoughts into words for them to hold us back; we only have to let them fester somewhere within our general attitudinal atmosphere.

Third, moving from generalized negativity to optimistic health means not just breaking old habits but actively establishing new ones. It takes time to develop new thought patterns, and having something specific to do each day—such as your Mind Fitness session with its seven specific steps—is an excellent way to make that new habit stick.

As we all know, developing new habits takes
time and attention, especially at first.

It takes effort to develop the habit of sitting down each day and quietly focusing on breathing, but it is usually more accessible than you may have expected. Once you make the time and start, relaxing and imagining your possibilities is enjoyable. If you aren't enjoying your images, change them so you *are*! Be sure you're having fun with your Mind Fitness. You are engaging in mental play—creating things in your mind exactly how you would ideally like to see them in your personality and daily activities.

Starting your program is a meaningful commitment to yourself. It begins the healing process and builds a new base for relating to ourselves and others. We are creating a new filter through which to see these things: a more positive one that makes everything in life fuller and more joyous. We are moving into a fuller flow in life, and we will find that everything is more accessible because we are more accepting and positive.

Our thoughts are what we call "an inside job."

Reflections

Take another deep conscious breath as you commit to a mental health practice that will balance and enliven your well-being.

Chapter 24

Seven Easy Parts

T HE FIRST STEP in this exercise—the one we must do even before the step listed as #1—is to *suspend judgment*. If we are used to resisting and reacting negatively to new things, there will be a temptation to say things like:

- "This will never work for me."
- "This is stupid. . . ."
- "I don't believe in this. It's just another 'positive thinking' trick."
- "It might work for other people, but I won't be able to do it right."

Just for now, try to give up opinions, decisions, judgments, or second-guessing, and follow the seven steps. This can be challenging for people who quickly judge and put down most things in life. We can begin to sabotage ourselves even before we begin . . . or we can take a more courageous attitude and start the healing before we start the seven steps. It's our choice.

Step 1: Stretching

Relaxing the body is the first step to calming the mind, and stretching is one of the best ways to release tension and bring oxygen into your body. Take a minute to stretch your body and release any tightness in your joints or muscles. Any easy stretches will do; here are some ideas:

- **Tiptoes:** Stand on your tiptoes and gently reach your hands and arms over your head. Stretch as if trying to reach the ceiling (or the stars). Hold this position for a moment and then lower your arms.

- **Shoulder Circles:** Bring your shoulders to your ears and lower them as you rotate your shoulder blades in circles. Shoulders have been called the "should do's"—we often use them to "carry our burdens." As you move and stretch your shoulders, imagine those "burdened" attitudes releasing and drifting out of your body into the air.

- **The Turtle:** This ancient Chinese stretch is healing for the nervous system. Lower your chin to your chest, feeling your spine lengthen as you inhale. Then, raise your chin and squeeze your shoulders up to your ears as you exhale. Lower your shoulders to a normal position and feel the decrease in tension. End by tilting your head from side to side, ear toward shoulder, to gently stretch your neck.

- **Arm Swinging:** Standing with your feet two to three feet apart, extend your arms out from the shoulders and swivel to the left, then the right. Swing way around so that you see behind you. Do this circular movement about ten times to release tension from the spine and put energy back into the hands. Be sure to stretch your face simultaneously by smiling and releasing any tension that's been held there.

- **The Cat:** The truly cat-like way to do this is to get down on your hands and knees on the floor (ideally, on the cushioning of a thick carpet or mat). Breathing in, stretch your spine and abdomen toward the floor, then try the other way, slowly rounding your lower back toward the ceiling. You can also do this standing by moving your lower back and your shoulders in opposite directions, slowly arching your spine forward and backward.

Try doing these exercises to shake off built-up tensions before sitting down. Do them all, or choose those that work best for you. You may know other stretches you like and find relaxing. These stretches take sixty seconds and make it much easier to relax mentally and emotionally once you sit down. They help us release the physical stress and tension, preparing us for mental stretching.

Step 2: Preparing

Do yourself the favor of unplugging your phone or switching off the ring. Do everything you can to eliminate intrusions and distractions. Some people keep a journal handy to note any insights they may get. Now sit down cross-legged on the floor, on a cushion if you can, or in a comfortable chair, with an erect posture and feet on the floor. As mentioned, lying down may make you sleepy since the alpha brain-wave state reached in relaxation is close to the edge of sleep. Sitting up makes achieving a relaxed but alert and wakeful state easier.

The value of having a particular place for your practice is that you begin to form a positive habit. The habit strengthens each time you sit in that place, draw a few deep breaths, and go through your relaxation, visualization, and affirmation exercises. It gets easier to reach and maintain that state of relaxation. You move more quickly through your visualizations and affirmations.

Whatever place you've chosen, please take a few moments to make it yours and settle in. Sit in that comfortable chair for a few minutes and tell yourself this is your time, a centering part of your day.

Step 3: Relaxing

This is when you become a human *being* rather than a human *doing*. Relaxation is like preparing the soil for planting the seeds of your growth and health. Think of this as the time to remove large rocks from your garden and prepare the rows for planting.

Close your eyes. Slowly focus on breathing and the quiet warmth of relaxation moving through your body. Consciously release any tensions as you become aware of them. Move through your body, relaxing your toes and the arches of your feet, calves, thighs, buttocks, abdomen, chest, shoulders, arms, hands, jaw, face, and skull. Replace any tightness with warmth and quiet.

Breathe full, deep breaths into your abdominal area. Focus on your breathing, perhaps even counting your breaths. Allow a sense of quietness to come over you. Tell yourself that you are permitting yourself to relax your body and mind for the next few minutes.

Go over your meditation for relaxation—bring to mind the pond image or another relaxation exercise you like—and tell yourself in words that you are now experiencing what it feels like to be entirely at peace, in harmony with yourself and the world. As you begin to know how this state feels, it will be easier to maintain it at other times during your day. Remember you are teaching yourself something new—a skill that can be used in many different situations—and there is no right or wrong way to do it.

Step 4: Intuitive Listening

Now that we have relaxed physically and mentally, we want to turn more inward. This is the time during the Mind Fitness sessions to listen quietly. This is your conscious mindfulness time. Listening inward is an active process. You listen to your heart beating within your body and then your breath as it enters and leaves your lungs. Become aware of your mind, its restlessness, inner chatter, and quiet moments. Through this listening, we can become aware of a deeper, more peaceful, wiser part of us. That is the soul level of intuition.

For many of us, "doing nothing" may be challenging initially. Your mind may be restless and flighty as it moves from one "essential" thought to another. That's fine. Please think of this as a time each day to shift your attention from the outer world to your inner world and let the process take shape. You allow the quiet to form within you as you open yourself up to any images, urges, flashes of intuition, insight, or natural knowing that may come to you. We have all had those moments of wisdom in which there is a significant shift in our thinking. It may be a new understanding that allows for forgiveness or an insight that causes us to change our direction radically. You are now proactively guiding yourself to a mental quieting level at which you are more likely to experience those moments of insight and intuitive understanding.

If nothing comes to you, relax and enjoy the quiet time without pressure about what you "should do" or " ought to be." New research tell us that this is a mindfulness practice in which you are doing precisely what is best for your overall health and well-being: Taking time to relax and de-stress, balancing your body and mind, and allowing your mind and body to rid themselves of tension. Maybe this is the "cleansing ritual" for the mind and muscles—think of it as soaking your mind in a nice hot bath for twenty minutes. Any way you look at it, you are doing precisely what you should do for optimal health and well-being.

With its symbols, intuition is a gateway to the inner unconscious, the source of our most powerful thoughts and urges. The intuition speaks softly but persistently. It does not scream or obsess: that is the ego's role. In most daily life, the ego's demands drown out the intuition's whispers. But when we sit quietly, relax, and turn our awareness inward, we can more readily receive feelings and insights from our intuition.

Step 5: Visualizing

The inner voice isn't just some ephemeral, passive, fleeting sense. It is the conduit through which we translate our intentions and inner strengths into goals and actions in the world. We may think of it as our true nature, our essence, the values part of us. From this authentic part, we come to understand what we truly want in our lives so that we can focus our attention and skills in that direction. Many spend a lifetime pursuing goals that really don't mean much to them. When we listen to inner thoughts, we tend to understand a more genuine part that allows us to express ourselves more honestly and authentically in the world. A fuller, purer energy carries us forward because our dreams and goals are ours.

Now that you are completely relaxed and at peace and have opened up to the intuitive self, it's time for a few minutes of visualizing. This is the proactive part of reflecting: You actively use the mind to mentally create pictures of how you ideally want to experience different things in your life. You use your focused imagination to experience the possibilities, the ideal—rather than just seeing the all-too-obvious problems within various areas and relationships in your life. You direct the mental movies from your ideal viewpoint so you can begin to focus in that direction in daily life.

Note: Before you begin your Mind Fitness sessions, you may want to create defined personal images to suit your wants and needs. Plan what you want to focus on to have a clear picture to start with in mind. This is especially true if you focus more on a particular life issue, such as health or a relationship. These might be visualizations repeated over many fitness sessions, as you would lift weights over an extended period.

On other days, you may do general visualizations for personal or emotional healing and expand on different aspects of yourself. You might form an image of the kind of person you want to be and focus on one or two elements of that change during your visualization. If you try to focus on too many things, your energy may get scattered, and the session won't be as effective. And remember, you do not *have* to plan anything; it's OK to discover what naturally comes to mind from the intuitive mind. Sometimes, the most unexpected thoughts and insights pop up in the quiet.

> ***When you heal one aspect of yourself,***
> ***you affect all aspects.***

See, feel, hear, and experience yourself responding to someone who has been a problem for you. See yourself handling the situation as you would ideally want to. See, feel, and experience yourself getting out of bed in the morning with exactly the attitude you want. See, feel, and experience yourself moving through your day, taking care of your daily tasks with lightness and a sense of humor. Give yourself a road map of how you would ideally feel and be.

If negative behaviors slip into your visualization, see and affirm yourself by stopping, realizing that is not where you want to be, and reroute that image and those words. Experience a love for yourself by taking the time and effort to release your limiting attitudes. You are teaching yourself new, more personally validating ways of thinking. Fill your visualizations with details and feelings. Make them as vivid and natural as you can. Know that you become what you imagine.

Step 6: Affirming

Affirmations work directly with visualizations. They are directed words of intention and direction that we give ourselves to help us stay on track. Affirmations are statements that take intuitive images, deeper understandings, and insights and translate them to make sense to the language-oriented human brain. Affirmations integrate imagery with verbal words.

Affirmations are also the emotionally felt "*I can!*" part of the visualization, the statement to our rational mind that the things we visualize are genuinely possible. Words give us clear directions. Positive words direct us to stop automatic mental chatter that can play continuously and automatically in our minds.

It's best to begin your affirmations while you are doing your imaging. While you are still visualizing, start to talk to yourself in a directed and purposeful way, using the statements of affirmation you have chosen. Give yourself a positive script to create these mental movies.

Verbal Clear Directions: You will find that just the right words of direction will surface from your intuition. Don't be afraid to try several statements and words until you sense the most powerful one. These short, positive phrases help keep the mind on track. We're replacing long-standing habits of mind, so we'll need to repeat the clarifying statement of intention and affirmation to get our minds going in the new direction. You know how easy it is to slip back into a habit. These statements help stop the automatic harmful habit and set you on the path of clear direction.

You may want to print your intentions on cards and leave them in various places in your home—on mirrors, on the refrigerator, or by your desk. It helps to add a little drawing or a visual symbol like a circle or square that will remind you of your intention to move on with your life. Goals are more accessible to memory when paired with a picture. As you hold these words in your mind, know that they have the power of your dreams behind them; they are clear, concise self-directions with no doubt that you can create them in your own life.

Step 7: Finishing

This is completing your workout, a time to return from your quiet world into the outer world. Wiggle your fingers and toes, open your eyes, and stretch your arms wide.

Congratulate and acknowledge yourself for having devoted this time and energy to your growth, happiness, and well-being. Know that you face the world with more resources and balance now than twenty minutes ago.

Remind yourself that attitudinal health improvement doesn't occur *only* in these quiet times. It becomes more a part of your life all the time, every day. You don't have to sit down with your eyes closed to "pump images" as bodybuilders pump iron. You'll have many opportunities each day to give yourself some quick affirmations, briefly flash a visual image of an event that you want to happen, or flood yourself with the experience of being the person you want to be. Over time, you will be able to do your mind lifts even while doing other activities that do not require 100 percent attention.

You may initially need to give your new and positive attitudes a great deal of attention. They are like infants in the beginning—unsteady and a little fragile. You are on the path to strengthen your new thinking so it can carry you rather than you carrying it. That is the transition you're looking for, which comes with perseverance.

You may feel awkward or uncomfortable the first few times you go through your Mind Fitness workout. You may have to stop and check on the steps at first. That's the newness of any approach to change, combined with any resistance you may encounter to quieting and perhaps even to changing yourself. Remember that this will pass. Everything will start to get much easier very quickly. You will start to feel more in charge and more creative. You will begin to see the results, and then the process of health and empowerment grows exciting. When you have the confidence that comes from success, your Mind Fitness work becomes very powerful.

Practicing consistently restructures the inner voice—from old, destructive habits into new, life-affirming thinking patterns.

We begin to experience changes in our lives and, more importantly, how we feel about ourselves and relate to others. Ideally, each day becomes a treasure rather than something we must get through. We begin living joyfully and creatively, no matter our daily activities. We begin to feel a light within us—the kind of active love that doesn't wait for things to happen but makes the most of each day. An inner peace and calm emerge.

Now, let's explore some visualizations people have found particularly useful.

Reflections

Read through the Seven Steps again to anchor them in your mind. Then do your practice in a way that fits for you.

Say "thank you" to yourself!

Chapter 25

Two Stories: Joan and Ben

Lᴇᴛ's ᴛᴀᴋᴇ ᴇxᴀᴍᴩʟᴇs of two kinds of life goals—one specific and one more general—and see how you might visualize and affirm each. Of course, the more specific you can get about your goals, the more likely you will be able to manifest them. But sometimes, we just aren't ready to get clear. It may take some time to work down from "Feeling better about myself" to "Being more positive at work" to "Not letting my boss, Ed, get to me when he asks me to work overtime."

Specific Goal Story: Joan's youngest child started college last fall, and she suddenly was rattling around the house, getting more bored and irritable by the day. While the kids were growing up, she had worked part-time, a year here and a year there, but had never found anything she particularly liked and never felt she could put much energy into her jobs. They were just ways to bring in some extra money and keep herself from going stir-crazy.

But now she was starting a whole new life and wanted a career to which she could devote the energy she'd given to the kids. The problem was she saw and labeled herself as "just a housewife" with few skills and no competitive edge. She had thought about getting a public relations or real estate job but knew she didn't have those skills and lacked the confidence to believe she could learn them.

After a few sessions focusing on her strengths and desires, Joan could see that she wasn't wholly unskilled and had tremendous organizational abilities. She could walk into any house or office and set things up so that they worked. She could also see that this skill could be used in an office manager position in public relations or real estate.

Still, she had her doubts. She hadn't had a full-time job since she'd married twenty years earlier, and she wasn't sure anyone would want to hire her.

When Joan came to the visualization part of her Mind Fitness workout, she let herself flow into an image of herself in an office—moving around with confidence, enjoying the respect of the people around her, contributing to what they were doing, and feeling the satisfaction that came from doing a good job.

She pictured what she was wearing and how it felt to sit at her desk, work with the various files, and talk with people who came by her desk. She took herself through the whole day, from arriving in the morning and taking off her coat, through the morning and lunchtime to the afternoon, and finally to leaving in the evening.

She saw what she did, and more importantly, she let herself realistically imagine the experience of going through that day. She felt the emotions, tasted the coffee, heard the various office sounds, saw the people moving around, and imagined everything as it would be if it were perfect.

After a week of visualizing this scene daily in increasing detail, accompanied by "I can do this" affirming words, Joan was ready to make some calls and start interviewing. She had spent the necessary time to sequence what would be asked of her and how she would feel about doing each task. She had slowed herself down enough to combine her left-brain sequencing and analyzing skills and her right-brain sensing and imaging skills to "try on" this experience in her mind.

The experience of successfully managing an office felt natural to her. She knew she could do it; an office would be lucky to have her.

> *It's often said that the unconscious does not distinguish between an imagined experience and one that happens.*

Joan was wise to pump images of confidence and remind her unconscious how competent she was before she had to go out and convince a prospective boss.

As Joan was visualizing, she might have used some of these affirmations:

- "I am a competent person who contributes to any group or set of circumstances," while she sees herself interacting within a group of imagined coworkers.
- "I am capable and particularly gifted with an ability to organize things," while she imagines herself organizing people and workloads.
- "When I interview for jobs, people sense my abilities and want to hire me," as she envisions herself sitting in an office during an interview.

General Direction Story: Ben was so low that all he could come up with as a goal for visualization was not to feel so terrible when he got up in the morning. He wasn't ill or hungover. He just had no energy or desire to get out of bed. For now, it wasn't even necessary for Ben to discover *why* he felt so awful; he just needed some relief.

Ben first had to switch his goal from "not feeling so terrible" to "feeling like something is worth getting out of bed for." Then, he had to decide what it would feel like to feel good about getting up in the morning.

Ben's visualization went like this. He entered his state of relaxation and imagined himself in bed before waking up. He saw himself sleeping peacefully and then beginning to stir. As he began to wake up, Ben became the man in the bed and imagined himself slowly coming to consciousness and becoming aware of the things around him. He saw the clock on his bedside table and the morning light starting to go through his bedroom curtain. He smelled the coffee in the kitchen downstairs and felt the soft, cool sheets against his arms.

He focused on this thinking. He thought about seeing a bird flying against the blue sky and visualized that bird until a smile started to spread across his face, and he began to get into that experience. Ben loved birds, so he used that image as "something worth getting out of bed for." He consciously thought about other nice things he could do that day and how he could make that particular Tuesday more pleasant for himself.

Ben had to be an actor. At first, he had to pretend to be more optimistic than he felt in the mornings. "Fake it, and you'll make it" became his motto. Over a month, it became more accessible for Ben to walk through this visualization. Soon, he no longer had to fake it; he moved through the visualization smoothly and effortlessly. He enjoyed it so much that he started doing the exact visualization as he woke up every morning. It wasn't long before he lived his images and even surprised himself by jumping out of bed enthusiastically one morning.

Along with his visualizations, Ben might have used affirmative ideas such as:

- "The first things I experience in the morning—the sheets, the smell of coffee, the sound of birds, the morning light—are all joys to me. I can get up and start doing something positive," while seeing himself doing precisely that.
- "I am ready for the day. I know I can make it a good one," while mentally rehearsing, looking out at the sunshine, and feeling good.
- "Cut the self-indulgent whining! I can look forward to getting involved in my life positively," as he imagines himself cutting a ribbon of whine and seeing a few of his good fortunes, such as his wife, home, and health.

Reflections

Take a moment to recall the words "to define is to create."

Using Joan's story, define a specific goal that you would like to create in your life.

Using Ben's story, define an attitude you would like to create that would lead you to a better place inside yourself.

PART 3

Building Steady Attitudes

Our attitudes determine how we view and go through life, so building steady attitudes is a major focus of healing negativity with Mind Fitness.

Chapter 26

Positive Momentum Images and Techniques

W E HAVE AN infinite number and variety of images at our disposal. The mind is limitless and can create constructive images for most situations or conditions if we let it. As we get into the new habit of forming images of love, goal fulfillment, and generosity, something compelling happens in our lives. The essential energy behind everything we do begins to change, to become unlocked, moving with more synergy. We feel more positive and connected as we sense we are increasingly in charge of our lives—at least on the inside—and have the intention and willingness to succeed and be happy. The filter through which we look at life becomes more giving, optimistic, and enthusiastic. We have a developing self-belief that things will work out for the highest good, even if we can't see it right now.

Once this process begins, it starts to feed on itself and snowball. One success breeds another. One loving thought or moment makes the next one easier. One act of kindness to ourselves and others grows into two or three.

We begin to build a positive momentum.

In time, we become more skilled at developing our self-direction, healing, and mastery images. They begin to bubble to the surface without effort because we are in closer contact with our inner voices and are more in touch with our authentic selves. Healthful images become available to us more automatically, replacing the old familiar habits of judgment and negativity.

But sometimes, before becoming masters of directed inner seeing or visualization, we need a jump start. The following visualizations are ones I've used with good results and ones that others have found successful and recommended to me. Some are general, and some are specific. As you read through them, find and use those that resonate with you. Perhaps some will prompt other ideas that relate specifically to your issues.

Remember to concentrate on your rhythms as you develop your images. If you are a person who likes experiencing things through sound, make sound or music a part of your images. If you like touching, make that an essential part of your images. Let yourself gravitate to what you most enjoy and use them to enhance your visualizations. Make each a sensual, solid experience that captivates you while in it.

Remember to draw on images and sensory experiences with deep and rich experiential meaning. You can mentally place yourself on a beach or a mountain, in a forest, skiing, sailing, or reading quietly by a fire. The scene's particulars aren't as crucial as *personal meaning* and the ability to bring deep *feelings* are.

Model Visualizations

These template or model visualizations are more than jump-starts for your images. They are practical tools to develop and keep available when you need quick help. When you succumb to a negative spin on the situation, having a familiar visualization handy can help you lift yourself out of it at a moment's notice.

When everything gets to you simultaneously—kids, boss, workload, even the weather—it's unrealistic to expect yourself to come up with a new, creative visualization designed just for those circumstances. Those images aren't always right at our fingertips in the middle of a bout with negativity and defeatism. We can keep ourselves centered and calm amid chaos by thinking ahead and preparing some images for emergencies.

We need these visualizations quickly retrievable on demand, as available as our address or the words to a song we love.

The power of template visualizations is that they are repeated often. We have already established the "grooves" in our mind that bring them into our experience and let us reap the benefits. These are off ered to clinicians or instructors who wish to read them to their students or you as an individual reader who perhaps wishes to record these visualizations and concentrate on seeing the images and feeling the sensations. These are just models, and I encourage you to think of other scenes that might be particularly meaningful to you.

Emptying Your Mental Closet

I walk into the closet of my mind. I notice all the dark, ill-fitting clothes scattered around the closet. Some hang off hangers, others are balled up on the floor, and some are doubled up on each other. I take a deep breath and throw out all the items that are no longer desirable. I start to really clean the house, as they say. And each time I toss something away, I say, "Goodbye, X," naming whatever negative characteristic I want to rid myself of. As I discard each old, dark piece of clothing that I no longer want or need, I feel a lightness and a quiet joy within me. Finally, I am doing what I have wanted to do for ages. Yes, it feels freeing to finally clean out the closet of unwanted habits and tendencies.

A Peaceful Visualization

I am seated in a lush garden with gentle hills and berry bushes. The flowers burst with brilliant purple, red, and yellow blossoms, and I feel a breeze on my sun-warmed face and arms. I get up and stroll around the garden, staying on the white stone pathway. I slowly move through the colorful flowers, stopping to smell the red ones and touching the petals of the blue blossoms. I feel a sense of complete harmony and tranquility fill my entire body and mind. I take a deep breath and know I am safe and at peace. With each breath, I feel peace touching my body, mind, and soul. The sweet, gentle air brings renewed serenity and harmony with each breath.

This visualization works well when you want to fill yourself with quiet, either because of a stressful situation or because you are now ready to sit down and relax deeply. The more you use it, the more quickly you'll reach a state of relaxation and peacefulness. Remember, the effects are cumulative.

Energy Visualizations

I have two favorite visualizations for energy:

1. Beam of Light. *I walk up to a brightly sparkling shaft of light and stand gazing into it. As I look into the beam of sparkling light, I take a deep breath and let go of all my physical and mental tensions. When I am ready, I lift my arms over my head as if doing a giant stretch. As I slowly lower them, I walk into the center of the shaft of light.*

I imagine taking the light into my body through my breath and all my pores, allowing it to fill me with a powerful energy. I concentrate on feeling the tingling in my cells and limbs. When I feel filled with energizing light, I open my eyes and affirm that this energy is now within me, and I am ready for whatever is next.

2. Springboard: *I stand on a giant springboard and begin to jump up and down, filled with delight and fun. Each time I jump higher and higher with my arms swinging, I feel filled with more energy to accomplish whatever I want.*

This is a visualization to "pump yourself up" and give yourself an extra burst of energy when needed. It is particularly effective for people who learn best through movement.

The Doorway Visualization

I begin by taking several deep breaths and see a doorway before me. Sometimes, I imagine it to be large and impressive; other times, it is simple and natural. It could be studded with jewels or made of simple bamboo, high and arching, or low and cozy. And the doorway can be different each time I approach it, depending on how I feel. I take a deep breath as I see the door.

Slowly, I imagine the door swings open. On the other side are health, creativity, love, healing, compassion, happiness, peacefulness, and how I ideally want to live my life. It's there waiting for me; I only have to walk through the door—I picture perfection.

I take another deep breath, step across the threshold, and enter the world of my dreams. I pause to look around and see exactly what is here.

What work am I doing?
Who are the people in my life?
How do I relate to them?
What do I feel like?
Can I let myself even imagine all that is peaceful and good?
As I breathe in one final time, I feel all of this is within me, and I am willing to accept it with a smile.

Reflections

Choose one or more of the model visualizations that may offer you direction. Change it in any way you find meaningful.

I personally use the Emptying My Mental Closet and the Doorway images as my often-to-go templates.

153

Chapter 27

You Are in Charge! Techniques That Work

Intentionally reliving events or experiences in the mind's eye so that they are how we want them to be is one of the most valuable tools of Mind Fitness and a potent way to use visualization. Reliving constructively joins imagination with logical and imagery skills and can be crucial in healing. Mental rehearsal, from the point of view of our ideal, holds a lot of value for us when it comes to learning and finding direction. It is a way of actually replacing negative experiences with positive ones. Remember, our unconscious can't distinguish between events that are imagined and those that happen.

> ***Reliving events in a more positive vein creates new and more positive grooves in our mental patterns.***

We can intentionally relive events in the past, in the present, and in the future. Reliving painful or adverse events from the past accomplishes two things: *healing* and *prevention*. Not only does reliving events more positively help heal our thoughts and feelings about the past event, but it can also help keep the problem from recurring. Understanding what happened, why it happened, and what we can do next time to prevent it is much more productive than beating ourselves up, feeling guilty, or blaming others.

Intentional Reliving Story: Every Saturday morning, Laura and her fourteen-year-old daughter Megan had a screaming battle about Megan cleaning her room. Over the last few months, Laura felt that this struggle had come to represent their entire relationship.

Megan was supposed to clean her room before she left the house each Saturday. But every Saturday, she came bounding down the stairs, dressed to go out, and would almost make it to the front door before Laura yelled, "Megan, did you clean your room?"

Sullen silence followed by one of an endless string of excuses: the football game, band practice, meeting a friend to study chemistry, or a sale at the department store. Laura was as infuriated by Megan's defiance as she was by the room not being clean, and the two of them launched into the regular Saturday morning screaming match.

When Laura started doing Mind Fitness, this was one of the first things she worked on. The fights with Megan on Saturday mornings left her drained and were beginning to set the tone for all their interactions.

Laura found some quiet time on Thursday afternoon and sat in her bedroom to do some intentional reliving. She played back what usually happened and looked to see what she was feeling and what Megan might be feeling. She formed a picture of how she would ideally like it to be.

First, she realized they weren't fighting about Megan cleaning her room but about Laura's control over Megan's life. Megan resented that she was still "under Laura's thumb" and that her activities were restricted on a weekend when her freedom was especially important to her. The more Megan resisted Laura's control, the more Laura needed to clamp down and *insist* on that control. It became a battle of wills—a test of who was in charge—that had little to do with whether or not Megan's room was clean.

Laura closed her eyes and began to imagine the Saturday morning scene as she would like it to unfold next time. Instead of waiting for Megan to come bounding down the stairs as usual on Saturday morning, dressed to go out, Laura saw herself sitting down with Megan on Friday after school and talking.

She pictured both calm and connected, willing to listen to one another's points of view. In her mind's eye, she saw herself working with Megan to come up with a solution to this problem of cleaning the room. Megan talked about how she hated having to do it on Saturday, and Laura asked her when she would like to do it. Laura didn't care *when* the room got cleaned and had just chosen Saturday because that's when *she* had cleaned her room as a teen. Megan said she wouldn't mind cleaning her room if she could do it on Thursday or Friday after school, and Laura thought that would be fine.

They both got what they wanted and didn't have to argue to make it happen. Having already gone through the entire scene in her imagination, Laura was ready to tackle the situation in "real life" several times and found that it unfolded almost exactly as it had in her imagination.

Intentional reliving can heal many kinds of hurts. It lets us *do* something about the questions:
- "How might I have handled that more graciously?"
- "What could I have done so that I felt better about that situation?"
- "How could we have avoided that fight?"
- "What might have allowed her to see my point of view and let me get a better look at hers?"

Each time we relive an event in our imagination, we heal the past and create a positive program for the future.

Stop, Cancel, Replace

As we become more aware, we learn to react quickly and can sometimes "relive" events *as they are happening* so that the negative attitudes and behaviors never have a chance to take root. When we notice ourselves starting down a negative or resistant path, we can:
- **STOP** the negative momentum by simply stopping whatever we are doing or thinking; pause for a moment to acknowledge that we are doing something we no longer want to do—something that does not benefit us. Now, we are taking a step to become self-directed. Then we . . .

- **CANCEL** the negative attitude or behavior. We say "Cancel" and make a strong hand motion, like a chopping motion in the air, to anchor cancellation in our minds. Finally, we . . .
- **REPLACE** the negative attitude or behavior with what we *do* want to say or think. We replace what we no longer wish to be doing with what is more supportive of us.

We don't always have the time to sit down, close our eyes, light a candle, start the music, and take several deep breaths before we do this. Saying "Cancel" can be done quickly and inconspicuously. If I find myself saying or thinking words from my old reactionary patterns, I say "Cancel," make a large or small chopping hand motion signifying my desire to cut that energy or thought, and then say it the new way. It takes only a moment.

Rod's Story: Rod thought that his father, Allan, had never gotten over Rod's decision to go to law school instead of trying for a career in pro football. Whenever they talked on the phone, Allan steered the conversation back to football, commenting on various teams and noting how much money different players were making. He never wanted to hear about Rod's law practice and fell silent when Rod brought up the subject.

As a result, nearly every time they spoke, they fought. Rod couldn't stand not being acknowledged by his father, and Allan couldn't stand considering the possibility that Rod had been right in not playing football.

Rod realized that he couldn't count on Allan changing and that if they were going to stop fighting, he had to be the one to do it. The triggers that prompted his negative outbursts were obvious; now, he just had to find a way to stop himself in time.

Rod prepared by intentionally reliving during his Mind Fitness workouts, imagining himself taking his father's backhanded criticism in stride. He focused on seeing his father with new understanding and loving forgiveness. Rod got clear on his position. He didn't want to become a doormat; he also didn't want to feel that he had to defend himself and get into a fight with his father every time they talked. He decided to take charge of how he viewed things and to give up wanting to change his father.

Sure enough, the next time Allan called, he started talking to Rod about the Bears game and how much money the new rookie was making. Rod's first instinct was to react and fight back, but instead, he took control of the situation. He told himself to STOP and CANCEL that negative pattern and replace it with understanding and love for his father. He let his father talk about the Bears and accepted him as he was. Later on, he was able to REPLACE it by changing the subject to something neutral.

It wasn't the last time Rod had to go through that conscious process, but this first success made the next one easier.

Monsters

We all have specific primal fears. They usually originated in childhood, when we felt helpless and victimized, and sometimes they have tremendous power over us. If we know what they are, we can work on them in our personalized time-out sessions and strip them of their power. By anticipating what will happen the next time a fear pops up and reliving the experience in advance, we can take increasing control of old unconscious patterns. We can do something about those monsters before they even come around.

My Monster Story: My monster found me when I was ten. He was the neighborhood bully, and my brother and I became the objects of his daily scorn. I remember the feeling I always got when he was around. I felt terrified, resentful, and victimized. Feeling helpless and victimized led to anger and hatred, and I felt engulfed in the waves of despair and vengeful thoughts. Any form of abuse—physical or mental—terrorizes and leaves deep emotional wounds.

That particular day, I was walking down a quiet street. Suddenly, I knew he was behind me; I could feel his presence. An overwhelming fear welled up inside me. When I walked faster, he walked faster. There was no place to hide, and I could feel his overpowering force beginning to swallow me up. As the moments ticked, I felt as helpless as a mouse in a cage about to be consumed. He caught up with me and blocked my way. The solid blow to my stomach was so quick, so frightening, and so

159

shocking that to this day, I have that same bodily sensation whenever I feel overwhelmed.

When I began practicing inner mind awareness, I found a way to deal with the fear and anger rooted in this early incident. I focus on reliving that experience with the bully in my imagination, becoming aware of my body's tightening and constricting. I then replace that terror and anger by consciously relaxing my body with my breath and concentrating on feelings and scenes of safety. The idea is to feel the anger and pain and then quickly replace those feelings with love, safety, and warmth. I focus on reprogramming my emotions by allowing myself to experience the old, negative ones and then giving them an overlay of positive ones that begin to take away the bully's power.

I create a bridge from the negative to the positive,
joining the two and quieting the old fear and anger
with today's feelings of safety and love.

When those old "bully feelings" come up, I feel bodily physical sensations in my body. When that happens, I quickly act to STOP, CANCEL, and REPLACE the old pattern with the new. It sounds mechanical, but knowing to do something mechanical when in emotional trouble is pragmatic and useful. Remember, you are not denying your feelings, but recognizing and acknowledging them, then replacing the old feelings with new templates. This technique can be used on other fearful symptoms. It's a matter of getting clear on your triggers, where they come from, and the fact that we can do something about them.

Watching for Pitfalls

We all have specific triggers that set off our brand of darkness—certain people, places, and things that tend to rob us of our positive outlook and make us resistant or cause us to put on the "gray-colored glasses." The trigger may be visiting a particular relative, being with certain friends, going out to certain restaurants or nightspots, or even the change of season from fall to winter.

It's essential to identify these negativity triggers so we can be on the lookout for them. The more aware we become of when we are likely to fall into negative thinking, the better we can avoid it. The blind person rarely stumbles on curbs because he makes a point of knowing where they are. In the same way, when we can identify the people and things that reactivate our negative patterns, we can either steer clear of them or be prepared to deal with them differently.

The better we know ourselves, the better we can manage and support our positive patterns.

Butterfly on My Shoulder

Exercising awareness and vigilance doesn't have to be complicated or unpleasant. A teacher once told me that I should go through my days as if there were a gentle and all-seeing butterfly on my shoulder that watched everything I thought, did, and said: the fair witness.

So I imagined a blue iridescent butterfly sitting on my shoulder who would observe how I thought about my family, my work, and my home. I would listen to my tone of voice with various people and watch what upset me.

The butterfly on my shoulder helped me become aware of how I was going about my daily living and where I was concentrating my energies—to see myself as I went through my day. The idea was not to beat myself up; that would be another form of personal negativity. The imagined butterfly would let me know my triggers for unwanted thoughts and actions. That was the information I needed if I wanted to begin healing myself.

Whenever I wasn't sure how the negativity was operating within me, I would sit quietly for a moment. It was amazing how quickly I began to spot—through the butterfly's eyes—my self-sabotaging attitudes. Whenever I saw something I wanted to change, I could intentionally relive it mentally in its ideal form. That gave me the map I needed to move toward my new destination.

Reflections

Choosing specific techniques that work for you is important so that you have them available when you need them. I often use the Stop/Cancel/ Replace technique. It's quick and very effective.

Try incorporating that Stopping Technique into your life as you become aware of negative speech or reactionary behaviors. Stop everything, Cancel it, Replace it with the image, and then affirm to yourself the way you want it said or done.

Try carrying the Butterfly on Your Shoulder for about a half hour one day. I think you be amazed at what you become aware of. Once you have tried it out, carry it around more often!

Chapter 28

More Techniques That Work: Negativity Breakers

Committing to healing personal negativity and embarking on a positive approach to mental and emotional care is essential in building a new life based on dynamically proactive love, health, and optimism.

You will probably notice some results right away. They may be big things like a new job or relationship or small things like having more energy in the morning, enjoying your time with the kids more, or not getting so upset in traffic. Some days, your new mental care orientation will seem like something magical that has utterly transformed your life. On other days, life may not feel too different from how it's always been.

Remember, making these kinds of dramatic and permanent changes takes time. Changes involving the habits of a lifetime don't usually happen overnight (although you shouldn't rule out that possibility). What you're after is a daily letting go of stress, followed by nourishment.

The following are techniques and exercises to remember. Some may seem silly, but that's fine—you can think of them as tricks for change. All of them are designed to work with your concentrated, twenty-minute Mind Fitness program and help build steady attitudes.

The "Remember" Sign

I have a friend in Hawaii with a huge banner across his living room. It says REMEMBER. It reminds him to be conscious of choosing his attitudes and actions rather than reacting automatically based on habits from the past.

Remembering—being mindful that we are the ones who choose what we do, say, and feel—is the cornerstone of building steady attitudes. We need to remember that we are in the mental driver's seat. We need to be aware of where our weak spots and negative tendencies are so that we can watch out for them and begin to heal them. That's easier if we also remember our higher self: the part of us that loves, grows, and is in balance.

Whenever I entered my friend's house, I felt calm and peaceful. Remembering to remember always brought me home within myself.

Negativity Breakers

These techniques help break the habit and accustomed energy of negative thinking and refocus that energy toward building a more self-supportive and expansive thinking habit. When we begin healing negativity, it's a lot like house cleaning. We throw away useless items and even items that were enjoyable at one time and replace them with new things that are more meaningful to us now. In this case, we're throwing out old thoughts and patterns of thinking. We're also renovating and redecorating with thought patterns that are loving, optimistic, and open to success in all areas. We may want to knock out some walls, add new doors or windows, or even build on a few new rooms with Mind Fitness.

I call the following techniques "Negativity Breakers" because they act like electrical circuit breakers to reduce the energy to old, negative habits. Most are physical actions that can be done to stop the flow of whatever is happening at the moment. After the negative flow has stopped, we can turn our attention to replacing it with something personally beneficial. Remember, you do not want to deny your feelings, but you want to move the energy to be more constructive. Asking yourself, "Is this good for me?" helps you determine how to proceed.

When you find yourself succumbing to negativity, try one of these Negativity Breakers to actively change the direction of your physical and mental energy:

Shake your hands hard as if you were shaking off water droplets. As you shake your hands, visualize negativity flying away from your fingertips. This exercise is amazingly effective for breaking up the tension and heaviness that is a symptom of negativity. It's like smashing a thin layer of ice on a pail of water.

Move your body. The physical act of moving your body will often move things around in your mind. When you start going down the Down road, get yourself into motion. Take a walk. Stretch. Turn on the music, dance, or do anything that changes your energy.

You may find at first that your body doesn't want to move or wants to move in small and stilted ways. Give yourself a few minutes and watch the changes. Your movements will take on breadth, shape, and rhythm, as will your thinking!

Your internal chemistry changes as your body becomes more accessible, animated, and alive. These physiological changes cause psychological changes and can move you out of the depression.

"No!" Another version of the Stop and Cancel refocusing exercise, this technique is rather dramatic and very effective. It also combines movement and words to state that you are no longer willing to accept the old obsessive negativity in your life. When you catch yourself thinking something negative, take a stand and say out loud to yourself as you lower your hands in a cutting gesture, "No! I will not accept that self-destructive thought anymore! I replace it with . . . [here, say your chosen replacement]."

There is nothing wrong with being dramatic. It usually works best. This technique underscores your power to *reject* self-destructive habits while creating new ones. The ability of self-imposed, constructive denial can also be a healing force, especially when barreling forward on a train of thought you have decided you no longer want to ride. Stop that train any way you can and deny its power over you. This dramatic

"No!" accompanied by a hand motion can work well with children and teenagers when you want to stop the flow of harmful or abusive energy with attention-getting drama.

Smile. It sounds ridiculous—as if you are pushing your deep inner feelings away—but again, you can use this technique when something has been identified, acknowledged, and accepted yet remains obsessive within your behavioral pattern. You want to re-channel your habitual reactive energy flow. If you can smile even when you don't want to, often you can change the focus of the thought. You may have to force the corners of your mouth up, stretch your cheeks back, and struggle to make it look like a genuine smile, but the results are actual. If you find this difficult, think of it not as a smile but as a facial expression. Making those physical movements changes how we think and feel. This is an extreme example of "fake it and you'll make it," but it can often work to redirect the automatic negative response.

Talk happy. This sounds silly, but try it. It is another version of "fake it, and you'll make it." When you are feeling down or depressed, try making liberal use of positive, happy words: "Yes, like, love, wonderful, happy, peaceful, fun, energizing, successful, good." You are taking charge of your negativity.

This won't be easy; your ego will fight you. It helps to prepare beforehand. Sit down when you feel great and write a list of positive words to pull out when you don't feel so great and they aren't exactly on the tip of your tongue. Again, it sounds silly, but not as foolish as rejecting an idea that works or living your life self-destructively.

Reserve negative comments. Let's not jump over an idea when someone comes up with it. Adopt a personal guideline that you will brainstorm about any idea for several minutes without anyone making any negative comments. Think of it as keeping a ball in the air for a few minutes. See if the idea has some merit as you "bounce it around" before you reject it entirely. It may be better than it first appears, or certain parts may be acceptable even if others are not. The important thing is that you will be teaching yourself to slow down your reactions.

Take a deep breath. This is a classic, used a great deal in Eastern practices. When things aren't going well, taking a deep breath serves as a reminder that situations can be turned around. It helps break up the energy, relaxes you, and sends oxygen to your brain. Many people began using this technique for physical benefits—relaxation and oxygenation—and found that they developed a positive pattern and association with it. When they take a deep breath, they not only get the physical benefits but associate the action with more positive outcomes and automatically move into a more expansive frame of mind.

Find and use a personal success symbol. Allow your creativity to be inspired. Use a picture, a little drawing, a symbol of some kind—just something visual that you associate with clear self-directed intentions of personal success to remind you to focus on moving into that frame of mind.

One woman in a group reported that when she stopped smoking, she went out and bought a sheet of little stickers in the shape of red apples. She stuck them up in various places in her house to remind her of that success and of the fact that if she could give up smoking, she could do anything. She associated the apple with the tale of William Tell splitting the apple on top of the boy's head. As a child, she'd been impressed by this impossible feat. She put the stickers on her bathroom mirror, refrigerator, desk lamp, computer, telephone, and nightstand. Whenever she saw those little red apples, she was reminded of a seemingly impossible feat—and that she was succeeding in that impossibility. She was reminded that she was doing this for herself and acknowledged the self-esteem she had gained from the victory. She began to feel she was also carrying that energy into other life areas.

Acknowledge other people. Whether it's an appreciation card to a coworker, a birthday message to a distant cousin, an "I love you" note to a parent or sibling, a thank-you to the guy with jumper cables who helped you start your car at midnight, or a letter of appreciation to be placed in someone's personnel file, letting other people know you appreciate them makes *you* feel good, too. It taps into that spirit of generosity, begins an upward spiral of energy, and comes back to you in mysterious ways.

Do a mini-visualization. The meeting is in five minutes. Suddenly, you feel unprepared and panicked. You've done your homework, but doubt somehow overwhelms you, and it seems as if everything will go wrong. You don't have time to sit down, close your eyes, and do a full-scale visualization, but you can take a deep breath, close your eyes for ten seconds, and get a picture of success.

Your quick mind lift might have you spin through the entire meeting on fast forward to get a sense of how you want things to feel while it's going on or envision the desired final result. Bringing the meeting into your mental sphere reminds you that you can succeed and don't have to be afraid. Mentally blast the situation with positive energy and let your positive attitude take over.

Reflections

I suggest you give each of the techniques offered in this chapter a try over the next period of time. See if one or two really speak to you as personal Negativity Breakers.

I often use Deep Breathing and consciously make myself Smile. They work for me.

Which ones are working for you?

Chapter 29

How Are You Treating You? Kindness to Ourselves

BUILDING STEADY ATTITUDES happens in two phases:

- Breaking the old, negative patterns, and
- Replacing them with new, more self-chosen ways of thinking and acting

Being actively kind to ourselves is part of the second phase. Most of us have not been raised to take gentle, loving care of ourselves. We've been discouraged from pampering ourselves; we were taught that such behavior is either selfish or a waste of time. But actively nourishing our souls and being gentle with our bodies demonstrates that we care about ourselves and want to replace some harsh treatment with kindness.

We can be kind to ourselves in many ways: physically, emotionally, and spiritually. The first step is to treat ourselves with more understanding and acceptance. We are human beings and have human frailties. None of us is perfect, and it's unrealistic to demand perfection of ourselves. We need to be as gentle and loving about our flaws as we are about the weaknesses of someone we love.

Another step is to give ourselves *permission to do things that feel good*—walking in the sunshine, sitting down with a cup of tea, watching a comedy on TV, stroking a child's hair, or simply sitting quietly doing nothing. Most of us don't permit ourselves to do these things simply because we want to do them. We walk because it's good exercise, drink tea because we need a rest to get back to work, watch comedy sitcoms because it's what the family is doing that night, and walk the dogs because we need to care for them. We need to calm down, stop thinking about what we should be doing all the time, and become aware of doing things just for the pleasure of doing them. That is called living in the present moment.

Negativity often takes a physical form when we don't take good care of ourselves—whether by eating poorly, not getting adequate exercise, or being mentally and emotionally out of balance. One of the themes of this book is that an attitude can be *learned* rather than just *passively caught.* Depriving ourselves of love and nurturing is a sure way to keep the cycle of illness and negativity going. It shows up in little ways. How do we put on hand cream or brush our teeth? How fast do we eat? Do we stop to taste and enjoy our food? These are all little indications to ourselves of how much—or how little—we are gentle and caring with ourselves.

We're often so busy and hurried that we don't realize how harsh and demanding we are. We don't even stop to consider what it would look like if we treated ourselves with more kindness and consideration.

I used to train grammar school teachers to be kinder to themselves. When they treated *themselves* more gently, amazing things started to happen in their classrooms. They began to treat the children with more gentleness as well. They demanded less perfection and were more caring and respectful of the children. When we permit ourselves to be more restful and gentle, we give that same permission to others. Once we begin the process, the cycle of kindliness and respect feeds off itself.

Story: A group participant told us, "I became aware of how ungentle I was with myself one day when a friend who was a hair stylist was cutting my hair. Before we started, she asked me to brush it. She watched and stopped me, saying, "Look how you're brushing your hair. You're not being very gentle or caring with yourself. You're not loving yourself very much."

"I was stunned. I stopped brushing and realized that she was right. I was tugging and pulling at my hair in a very unthinking and rough manner.

I realized that this was how I treated myself in many areas of life—that moment of realization opened up a whole new path for me. It was the beginning of being more aware and loving with myself and, therefore, with others. I started moving more slowly and gently, brushing my hair instead of attacking it. I began to see other parts of my life where I could treat myself more kindly. Instead of taking showers, I started taking baths more frequently, enjoying the time I was actively caring for myself. I allowed myself to engage in my hobbies more often, spend more time with my family, sit by the fire in the evening, and enjoy other simple pleasures. Each year, I am learning to give myself more permission to be kind to myself and honor the higher self within me. What I am learning is that it is a continual process."

Being kind to ourselves on all levels is one of the most important things we can do to build steady attitudes. It is a conscious act and one that is essential for healing. As we are more nurturing with ourselves, we become more considerate and kinder to other people. We have fewer judgments and more compassion. It's easier to see what it would feel like to be in another person's position. We develop more genuine affection for people and enjoy them more. We begin a cycle of love that nurtures all of us—and there is nothing like love to turn a negative filter into a positive one. That is where giving and receiving start to blend.

Spiritual Nurturing

We sincerely need to nurture ourselves on a spiritual level. Treating ourselves to a gift now and then, taking a long weekend, reading a good book, saying "No" to another obligation, taking time out to do a sport or activity that we like—all these things nourish us physically and mentally. Nurturing our spirit adds a whole new and critically important dimension to our life journeys. It means taking the time to appreciate our connection with the unknowable, the mysterious nature, and everything around us.

We may admire a flower, watch a stream as it flows downhill, or watch the sun sink into the ocean. If you're in a city, you may watch a raindrop on the window, see a tree overhead, or imagine connecting with people on a heart level while walking down the street. We direct ourselves to see over the personality, the racial, the economic, and job-related selves and extend to others in a new and more eternal way. Our inner being naturally comes to life when we consciously stop to realize our connection with something larger than ourselves and remind ourselves that we are part of a greater whole. As we stop to connect with the mystery of all of life in *all* its various and unique forms, living for centuries on this planet, all doing the same biological things in many diverse ways, we tap into awe that begins to help us overcome our little personalities and touch that more profound, more eternal part of ourselves.

> *There are many forms of inner quieting;*
> *only you will know which is best for you.*

You may choose a formal method taught for centuries or sit quietly with yourself for a few minutes each day, focusing on inner calm and peace. No form of quiet awareness is better than another. What counts is the peace, energy, and love that you find within yourself as a result. This is a time to be with your deeper self and connect with something other than day-to-day living. It is where you find quiet and can just let things be and appreciate them. Enjoying a meal is nourishment for the body. Reading or engaging in a challenging conversation is nourishment for the mind. Inwardly silencing yourself is nourishment for the spirit. It is the essence of any personal Mind Fitness program.

A Review: When you first sit down to spend this quiet time with yourself, you may find that all your attention is on your body. You may feel tension in various spots and need deep abdominal breathing to release it.

When your body has relaxed, shift your attention and begin to quiet your mind, slowly asking it to relinquish its chatter and just be still. Try repeating a word or phrase that has personal meaning to you. This may be a formal mantra given to you by a teacher or some word such as "Peace" that you repeat to yourself until your mind quietens. Each time your attention wanders, gently bring it back to the phrase. Don't beat yourself up if you get distracted. This is an exercise in forgiveness, concentration, and acceptance.

The easiest and best way to quiet the mind is to watch your breathing. Be aware of each breath as it enters and leaves your lower abdomen. You can count the breaths or see the air stream as a ribbon of color.

Another good way to quiet a chattering mind is to imagine yourself sitting by the edge of a pond or river, resting as the sun and the quieting forces of nature work their magic on you. You may have a template visualization that you use to move into a relaxed state.

When the body and mind are finally at peace, rest and allow yourself to merge with your concept of the infinite; at this point, I feel a great richness pour over me like honey, and there seems to be no difference between my inside and my outside. I feel at one with myself and with everything else. There is no movement or chatter.

The more I practice mindful inner quieting, the better it feels and the more centered and calm I become in my daily life.

I feel more integrated on all levels:
physical, mental, emotional, and spiritual.

Inner quieting or meditation doesn't have to be anything mystical. It is simply a time each day for centering, quietness, and relaxation of body and mind, a time for making contact with the subtle parts of yourself and reminding yourself that you are connected with all of life. It is the aware inner-listening part of Mind Fitness. The quieting allows the intuition to take form within your conscious mind.

Explore various types of inner quieting, or make up a mindful meditation for yourself and practice a few minutes daily. You will notice a difference, and it will enhance the focusing work you do with the more active parts of Mind Fitness.

Reflections

Kindness to yourself and others is important to a sense of well-being. Look for opportunities to offer yourself and others a moment or gesture of kindness as you go through your days. Notice when you are offered the same. What a nice feeling that is!

Look for moments of connection with nature, people, and yourself. Feel a sense of gladness roll over you in those moments.

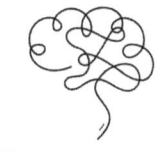

Chapter 30

"You're So Fine!"
Self-Acknowledgment

Acknowledgment is a positive force, whether directed toward others or ourselves. There can rarely be too much of it. Self-acknowledgement or praise is often not taught when we are children, so you may need some practice. You may need to consciously seek out your good deeds, good thoughts, and attitudes and inwardly praise yourself for developing and nurturing them.

Most of us have had to work to develop the positive aspects of our lives, and we deserve credit and acknowledgment. Praise is the best way to make things grow. If we want more positive thoughts, words, and actions in our lives, we need build on what we already have by acknowledging and praising the positives already there.

Another aspect of acknowledgment is to become aware of particularly fulfilling moments and appreciate and build upon them. We must highlight to ourselves those times and the people with whom we share those moments. It's usually much easier to be critical and judge what isn't working than it is to seek out the positive, especially in ourselves. The inability to compliment ourselves and others is a clear symptom of lack of self-appreciation . . . another cornerstone of personal negativity.

If acknowledgment of yourself or others is difficult, practice imagining yourself in a situation in which you are acknowledging. In your mind, imagine and live how you respond to positive reflections and words. How do others react when you acknowledge them? What is the ultimate result of the praise you give them and yourself? Do all this in your imagination as you shift from being one person to another.

Acknowledgment and criticism are both habits.

Since it is the nature of human beings to put attention on ourselves, we will probably have one habit or the other, depending on how we view ourselves. Since we can choose, it serves us better to choose acknowledgment. As part of the personal negativity pattern, we're often quick to criticize ourselves but much slower to acknowledge a goal achieved, an attitude change, or a more positive frame of mind. Sometimes, we work for years toward something and hardly ever bother to compliment ourselves once we have achieved it.

Recognizing the higher and more positive aspects of ourselves is a key to personal development. We need strokes to thrive, and we don't want to always count on getting them from other people. Part of becoming self-determined is learning to provide for ourselves and to have fun doing it. Developing the habit of acknowledging yourself healthily goes a long way toward replacing the habit of self-criticism and is an integral part of exchanging the negative filter for a positive one.

Mind Lifts

Remember mind lifts—those brief "pumping images" sessions we can do several times daily? Mind lifts are like lifts done with weights in the gym. They are quick repetitions that *build attitudinal muscles* and shape them to fit our visions. We can "lift" these whenever we think about it and want to take a hand in shaping our lives. Mind lifts help us work toward our goals and keep our energy and focus where we want them to be—whether that means pushing our enthusiasm a little higher or letting ourselves relax into a quiet time.

We can use images of goals achieved, relationships, appreciated love in bloom, happiness enjoyed, even the good fortune of sunshine . . . anything we want. The important thing is to feel the feelings. Some examples:

Images of Happiness: Most of us have never taken the time to consider what our lives would look and feel like if we were happy. During one of your meditation or Mind Fitness sessions, visualize yourself as a happy, fulfilled person. What would you be doing?

- Who would you be with?
- How would you feel?
- What would you look like?
- What would you be wearing?
- What would your attitude be?
- What would your life look like?

Once you have a clear picture of what happiness might look and feel like, you can flash on it as a mind lift at any time and bring it closer to reality. It might be playing with your children or grandchildren, swimming, lying in a hammock, taking a walk, cutting a flower, getting a massage, drinking a glass of water, having a good conversation, hugging a parent, or polishing a beloved car or table . . . pick a moment in life that you can feel is a happy moment and make that your go-to image of happiness.

Images of Love: Now, create some images of love. It can be romantic, friendship, family, or any form of love you choose. Sometimes, it is true that the most unconditional love is for a pet.

- Who is there with you?
- How do you feel?
- What do you want for this person (or pet)?
- For yourself?
- What is the texture of your relationship?
- Where is it going?
- What are the results of your love in both of your lives?

Images of Job Fulfillment: Do the same type of mental play, but this time, focus on what you would ideally like to see happen in your job. It can be a paid job, a volunteer job, a hobby, or even the "job" of being a mate, parent, or caregiver.

- What are the basic demands of the job?
- How are you handling the demands and challenges?
- Who is with you?
- What kind of attitude do you have?

- How much self-acknowledgement are you giving yourself?
- How much acknowledgment do you ideally want from your coworkers?

Make up meaningful mind lifts for work, sports, artistic endeavors, health, and any area you want to grow. Use the mental flashes frequently.

Remember, attitudes are like muscles. They only stay
strong and healthy when they are used and exercised.

A Way of Life

Building steady attitudes, like sticking with a regular fitness program, takes patience and perseverance. Inner mind work and self-direction are more than exercises we do for a few minutes by ourselves each day. The goal is to make new, positive habits a way of life. Building steady attitudes means that regardless of the daily ups and downs, we endeavor to hold ourselves on an even keel—a steadiness that is generally upbeat and generous, not falling prey to abrupt shifts in mood or long depression. We stay awake and aware.

We focus on life's opportunities because we have chosen to live a new consciousness and way of relating to life. The classic test of whether you're an optimist or a pessimist asks whether you see a glass of water as half full or half empty. Which way do you choose to go through life? We always have the choice. We can make optimism as natural a response as pessimism may be for us today if we decide to be more light-hearted every day. Seriousness is not all it's cracked up to be.

I want to emphasize again that as we go through life, we will encounter severe "downdrafts." We can't control events outside ourselves, but we *can choose how we feel about those events* and react to them. How we feel at any given moment has less to do with external events than *how we relate to ourselves* and the attitudes we foster within ourselves. Often, it is the people who have had little hardship in their lives who have the most Down, harsh, and self-indulgent attitudes—who see the glass as half-empty—while others who have had to survive grave life difficulties have come to terms with dark times and learned to focus on that half-full glass of water. When our point of concentration becomes *internal* rather than *external*, we gain power over our own lives.

How we go through life is an inside job.

Personal to Global

The positive orientation of healthier people ripples out from individuals, families, communities, and even into the world. It is a growing evolution in consciousness. Imagine the potential of six billion people free to construct dreams, goals, and visions, to imagine the very best for themselves and the world, everyone participating in a compassionate and mentally healthy form of thinking and consciousness. (Since this book was first written, the world population has increased from six billion to over eight billion people in 2023.) It seems far-fetched, but if we cannot envision it even in quiet prayer and thought, we surely will not create it.

Imagine what relationships among people and nations could be like. People could express the deep connection and love instead of interactions being clouded by fear and separation. We could become the family of humankind caring for ourselves, each other, and the Earth we live on. Idealistic compared to today's realities? Of course.

It can only manifest if we can imagine it, speak
of it, and act upon interactions daily.

I am always amazed at how quickly we humans respond to the positive. I was reminded of this by a documentary on Mother Theresa. The incident occurred years ago, but it still has such power today. A boy in Beirut had been so shell-shocked that his entire soul seemed to have retreated deep within his body. He just lay on his side shaking, utterly unresponsive to anything, staring with eyes empty from the horror he had seen around him. Mother Theresa started to stroke this boy's head and back, and within just a few minutes, he stopped shaking and turned his eyes and hand toward the source of this loving touch. I was astonished that a child so profoundly contracted would respond quickly to a simple loving touch.

We have all been shell-shocked by our battles, and we all respond to the positive. We have the ability to touch ourselves and one another in Mother's same way with our love. A smile heals like sunlight; a touch heals the heart. As we grow and actively empower ourselves, that smile and touch gets closer to the surface—more available to us and the people around us.

Those of us who live relatively free of persecution, abject poverty, and constant physical danger have the responsibility to pioneer and actively support this next step in human evolution and consciousness. We are privileged to turn our minds and hearts to personal healing and growth and reach out to our neighbors in compassion and justice.

Once we have moved beyond our emotional and physical survival, we can turn our creativity toward contributing to others through our chosen attitudes and actions. How we go through the world speaks volumes. The desire to love and contribute to one another is a primal human urge. The commitment to consciously design our life around compassion and love is a personal commitment to ourselves and others. It might mean something as simple as devoting a few minutes a day to imagining yourself and the world at peace or imagining a change of understanding, empowering humans to live together on this planet with equal respect and justice.

"The possible human is inclined toward fairness, goodness, and excellence. When we create enough individuals so inclined, we then create societies capable of fairness, goodness, and excellence."
~ **James Comer, Yale University**

Recommended Books

This is the list of books I found helpful and enjoyable when writing this book. They are classics. You will see an extensive reference section in the newest Mind Fitness book, *Mind Fitness: A Guide to Elevating Mental Health.*

The Art of Happiness: A Handbook for Living. His Holiness the Dalai Lama and Howard C. Cutler, M.D. Riverhead Books.

Beyond the Relaxation Response: How to Harness the Healing Power of Your Personal Beliefs. Herbert Benson, M.D., and William Proctor. Berkley Publishing Group.

Change Your Mind, Change Your Life: Concepts in Attitudinal Healing. Gerald G. Jampolsky, M.D., and Diane V. Cirincione. Bantam Books.

Creative Imagery: How to Visualize in All Five Senses. William Fezler, Ph.D. Simon & Schuster.

Creative Visualization. Shakti Gawain. Bantam Books.

Emotional Intelligence: Why It Can Matter More than IQ. Daniel P. Goleman. Bantam Books.

Fire in the Soul: A New Psychology of Spiritual Optimism. Joan Borysenko. Warner Books.

The Healer Within: The New Medicine of Mind and Body. Steven Locke, M.D., and Douglas Colligan. Dutton/Plume.

Imagery in Healing: Shamanism & Modern Medicine. Jeanne Achterberg. Shambhala Publications.

Living Simply Through the Day: Spiritual Survival in a Complex Age. Tilden Edwards. Paulist Press.

Love and Will. Rollo May. Delta.

Love Is Letting Go of Fear. Gerald G. Jampolsky. Celestial Arts Publishing Company.

The Miracle of Mindfulness: A Manual on Meditation. Thich Nhat Hanh, translated by Mobi Ho. Beacon Press.

Myths to Live By. Joseph Campbell. Viking Penguin Books.

The Relaxation Response. Herbert Benson, M.D. with Miriam Z. Klipper. Wholesale.

The Relaxation & Stress Reduction Workbook. Martha Davis. New Harbinger.

Sabbath: Restoring the Sacred Rhythm of Rest & Delight. Wayne Muller. Bantam Books.

The Seat of the Soul. Gary Zukav. Simon & Schuster.

Toward a Psychology of Being. Abraham H. Maslow, Ph.D. John Wiley & Sons.

Wishing Well: Making Your Every Wish Come True. Paul Pearsall. Hyperion.

Your Maximum Mind. Herbert Benson, M.D., and William Proctor. Times Books.

Discussion Questions

I sincerely hope you found *The Upside of Being Down: Healing the Dis-Ease of Negativity with Mind Fitness* a motivational read and that you learned that no matter how "Down" you feel, you can still discover your "Up Side" with practical tools to cultivate your mental well-being.

It is my hope that this book is read by individuals and is used by book groups, schools, and clinics as a learning model supporting mental health along with the rest of the books in the Mind Fitness series. The questions below were written to facilitate healthy conversations on various perspectives to enhance further understanding of the lessons learned.

Feel free to tailor these questions to your group's preferences and discussion style.

I encourage you to share pictures of your group or your favorite reading spot with me. I also appreciate your book review on your preferred retailer's website!

Wishing you fruitful discussions,

Joy Watson

1. Reflect on Your Mindset: After reading the book, take a moment to reflect on your own mindset. Are there specific negative thinking patterns you've identified in yourself? How do you currently approach challenges and setbacks?

2. Personal Application: The author encourages readers to embark on their own personal mental training. What specific Mind Fitness exercises or techniques resonate with you, and how might you incorporate them into your daily life?

3. Shift in Focus: The book emphasizes shifting focus from external factors to internal empowerment. Can you share an experience from your life where changing your perspective led

to a more positive outcome?

4. Creating Positive Habits: Chapter 13 discusses the three stages of healing. Which stage do you find yourself in, and what steps can you take to progress through these stages toward a more positive mindset?

5. Affirmations and Visualization: Chapters 18 and 20 introduce the power of affirmations and visualization. Have you ever used affirmations or visualization techniques in your life? How do you think incorporating these practices can impact your mindset?

6. The Payoffs of Positivity: In Chapter 12, the author discusses the payoffs of choosing a positive focus. Can you share an example from your life where choosing a positive focus made a significant difference?

7. Overcoming Challenges: Chapter 11 identifies different symptoms of dis-ease, such as defeatism, anger, and control issues. Can you relate any of these symptoms to personal experiences or challenges? How might the book's strategies be applied in those situations?

8. Mind Fitness for Healing: Part 2 focuses on Mind Fitness for healing. Which chapter or exercise stood out to you the most in this section, and how do you think it can contribute to mental well-being?

9. Building Steady Attitudes: Chapter 26 introduces positive momentum images and techniques. How can incorporating positive momentum images into your daily life contribute to building a more positive attitude?

10. Self-Kindness: Chapter 29 discusses the importance of kindness to ourselves. In what ways do you currently practice self-kindness, and how can you enhance or expand these practices based on the book's insights?

About The Author

Joy Watson, M.Ed., has worked as an international communications and learning consultant in business, education, and health. As the principal consultant of Mind Fitness International, she developed the integrated educational-health methodology known as Mind Fitness. She has designed communication programs to maximize human potential, personal and team success, and wellness, and has conducted seminars on Mind Fitness for a range of clients. As a human development educator, Joy holds degrees in sociology and speech and language pathology from Boston University. She is the author of multiple books on the subject of Mind Fitness: *Mind Fitness: A Guide to Elevating Mental Health*, *The Up Side of Being Down: From Stress to Sanity*, and she co-authored *The Mind Fitness Program for Esteem and Excellence*, designed for children.

Thank you for reading *The Up Side of Being Down: Healing the Dis-Ease of Negativity with Mind Fitness*. This is the first in a series of Mind Fitness books I hope you will enjoy.

May the practical tools within these pages be your companion on the path to cultivating lasting mental well-being. If you're eager to delve even deeper into the transformative world of Mind Fitness, I invite you to explore the website: www.mindfitnessbooks.com